ARE WE THERE YET?

JOHN MCLEAN

ISBN 979-8-89243-224-5 (paperback)
ISBN 979-8-89243-225-2 (digital)

Copyright © 2024 by John McLean

All rights reserved. No part of this publication may be reproduced, distributed, or transmitted in any form or by any means, including photocopying, recording, or other electronic or mechanical methods without the prior written permission of the publisher. For permission requests, solicit the publisher via the address below.

Christian Faith Publishing
832 Park Avenue
Meadville, PA 16335
www.christianfaithpublishing.com

Printed in the United States of America

Contents

Introduction		v
Chapter 1:	The Journey	1
Chapter 2:	The First Step	3
Chapter 3:	The Word	7
Chapter 4:	The Holy Spirit	11
Chapter 5:	Spirit, Soul, and Body	17
Chapter 6:	About Covenants	22
Chapter 7:	Benefits	27
Chapter 8:	Understanding Grace	31
Chapter 9:	Understanding Faith	35
Chapter 10:	Mind the Mouth	39
Chapter 11:	Confidence	43
Chapter 12:	Prayer	47
Chapter 13:	Giving	52
Chapter 14:	Worship	56
Chapter 15:	Fasting	59
Chapter 16:	Serving	63
Chapter 17:	Empathy	68
Chapter 18:	Religion and Works	72
Chapter 19:	Where Is There?	75
Chapter 20:	Persecution	79
Chapter 21:	Keep It Simple	83
Chapter 22:	One Day We'll Know	86

Appendix 89
    The Sacraments—Baptism and Communion 89
    The Roman's Road 93
    Emergency Numbers 93
    Bible Overview 97
    Rightly Divide 109

INTRODUCTION

The decision to follow Jesus is ultimately the most important decision that any of us ever make. The impact will not only be felt immediately, but throughout the rest of our lives and much further than even that. This decision will also be a big part of whatever legacy we leave behind us. It is my sole desire to help and encourage people with this decision, which is the purpose of this book.

At this point, it is advised that the reader skip to the twenty-second chapter of this book, One Day We'll Know. This will help put into perspective the things that I write. "In the fundamentals of the faith, we have unity. In the nonfundamentals of the faith, we have liberty. And in all things, we have love."

Please do not see my words as absolute fact—I only consider the Bible to be that. Many of the things written here are my observations, understandings, and opinions. The Bible stands on its own. Different people's observations, understandings, and opinions may vary. Many different churches have different doctrines or a published list of what they believe. Some of those doctrines may differ a little with what I write. Don't let that be a hindrance. We each arrive at our own understandings and opinions. We each develop a personal relationship with a loving God.

Move forward, be blessed, and be fruitful. Life may be full of troubles regardless of our best decisions. But with faith in Jesus, and an understanding of what that offers, those troubles can be overcome. I was such a one who made many bad decisions. At the age of forty, I was homeless, broke, and hungry. God told me to, "Read My Word." (I took that to mean that He wanted me to read the Bible.) I did and that changed my life. Gradually, my circumstances changed, but something inside of me changed right away. I had joy in unhappy times. I had peace in times of conflict. And I had love for people whom I otherwise did not necessarily like.

Becoming a Christian, getting saved, getting born again, or however we want to describe it, is much more than just whether we go to heaven or hell when we die. This decision will have a profound impact on our lives and our legacies. I would encourage anyone to let go of all preconceptions about this choice and go into this with eyes wide open. Know that God loves us and wants the best for each of us. As a matter of fact, what is described in the Bible and in this book is the greatest love story of all times. God has paid dearly so that we can lead a blessed and fruitful life.

Chapter 1

The Journey

Life and the good things that we desire of it is not a destination but a journey. We would never stand in line and pay for a ticket to sit in a crowded stadium to just hear someone tell us what the final score was. No. We want to behold the spectacle of the game and experience the drama of each moment.

Of course, we want our team to win. The same is true in life. We want to win. Winning is the process of overcoming obstacles to accomplish a desired goal. The greater the obstacles, the greater the sense of accomplishment will be. Life requires courage and perseverance. It requires utilizing the strengths and qualities we were born with plus a lot of extra effort on our own. And it takes time—a lifetime!

A simple overview of the science of physics tells us that if an object exists in one place and it is moved to another place it requires work. Some form of energy is required to accomplish that work. If where and how we are now is not all that we want in life, we need to get somewhere else. This too requires some work.

Sometimes the long-range goal is clear, but the intermediate steps are not yet known. Then again, sometimes the ultimate goal is unclear, but we know the general direction and what our next step is. Either way, movement is required. We must begin where we are and just start moving. When we keep moving, step after step, eventually we develop some momentum.

The obstacles that we face may change, and sometimes we must change our strategies to deal with that. If we keep our goals in mind, we can deal with those changes and maintain our momentum. I love to see a dog running in tall grass. They jump up to see where they are and then run some more. Eventually, they get through after constantly running and also checking to see where they are going.

Balance is important also. We can burn ourselves out if we don't get rest in between times of exertion. As we go, we find the balance that works for us. It serves no purpose to work, work, work to buy a big house for the family, only to find that we're never home to enjoy that house or family. Our kids grow up wishing they could have spent some time with us. Working extra hours is sometimes required, but I caution anyone to not let that become a lifestyle. A friend used to tell me that he worked to live, but he did not live to work.

Preparation is a factor, but it can also be a distraction. It is better to dive into something and figure it out as we go than to spend all our time and effort to prepare for something we never do. Reading books, getting a college degree, watching videos, lifting weights, running, and practicing the piano are all great things to do. However, if that is all we do, we don't get anywhere. That represents energy spent and no work actually done. Remember that we want to get somewhere or do something and not just be something or have something.

This book is designed to help anyone visualize the process of accomplishment and help him have a successful and enjoyable journey. None of us are in this alone, or at least should not be. Great help is available. When we first get started, we have no idea about just how great that help can be, or how it becomes available. My purpose in writing this book is to help anyone get acquainted with the greatest help of all.

Chapter 2

The First Step

There are some fundamental things to understand before any real progress is made. The very nature of life or the world we live in can be mysterious at first. A critical first step is to realize that there is a God. The world did not just pop into existence on its own. The things we see around us are not the result of a series of random accidents.

The intricacy of our own bodies should give us a clue. The way that plants draw carbon dioxide from the atmosphere and generate oxygen, and at the same time animals breathe oxygen and exhale carbon dioxide should tell us something. The evidence is all around us that this world, all plants and animals and the universe at large have been intelligently designed and created. That creator is God.

The nature of God is something that is also mysterious at first. When we think of someone who is all-knowing and all-powerful, it can be scary because we know that we are neither of those things. But when we realize that He is a loving God Who wants to bless us, we become less fearful and more grateful. This knowledge of God is available to all of us to whatever degree we desire. One of the best sources of that knowledge is the Bible.

I want to start with what is perhaps the most recognizable verse of the Bible, John 3:16. It says, "For God so loved the world that He gave His only begotten Son that whosoever believes in Him shall not perish but have everlasting life." This is a great starting point. The foundational points here are that God is, God loves, God gives, and God does not want us to perish.

Who is God? To begin with, He is the creator of the universe. He is the one who made everything that is. And He loves us. We tend to look at God and think that He loves according to our concept of love. But the Bible says that "God is love" (1 John 4:8). To understand God is to understand love. God so loved the world that He gave His only begotten Son. Who is that? That is Jesus.

Every year at Christmastime, we are exposed, in a variety of ways, to the story of the birth of Jesus. And every year at Easter time we hear about Jesus dying on a cross and then rising from the grave. This is where it gets really interesting. What was that all about? Let me explain in a nutshell and get our life journey going started on the right foot.

Not only is God almighty, He is absolutely pure. He has very high standards for purity. This purity applies to our conduct in business and personal life. Any failure therein is referred to as sin. Adam sinned when he disobeyed God and ate of a certain tree, and since then, every person who has ever lived has sinned as well. "There is none righteous, no not one" (Rom. 3:10). "For all have sinned and fall short of the glory of God" (Rom. 3:23). "For the wages of sin is death, but the gift of God is eternal life in Christ Jesus our Lord" (Rom. 6:23).

It is as if breaking any law is a capital offense, and we are all found guilty. But someone who was not guilty of any offense stepped in to pay the price for us. That is what the "Jesus on the cross" stuff is all about. Those wages of our sin were paid for with the death of Jesus on that cross. With our debt paid, we can now live free from guilt and the worry of eventual prosecution—the case is now closed.

Going back to John 3:16, "whosoever" means anybody. That means anyone and everyone we know. That does not mean just church people or just nice people. That means that felons, drug addicts, or anyone else are not excluded. Whoever means anyone. That is, anyone who believes. "That if you confess with your mouth the Lord Jesus and believe in your heart that God raised Him from the dead, you will be saved. For with the heart one believes unto righteousness and with the mouth confession is made unto salvation" (Rom. 10:9–10). This is called "The Gospel," which simply means "good news."

A great example of this is found toward the end of the Gospel of Luke. While Jesus was hanging on the cross, there were a couple other men hanging on crosses also. These men were guilty of some capital crime and were serving their just punishment according to the Roman law. One of them said to Jesus, "Lord, remember me when You come into Your kingdom" (Luke 23:42). To which Jesus replied, "Assuredly, I say to you, today you will be with Me in paradise" (Luke 23:43).

This was not a good or nice man. He didn't go to church, pay tithes, pray, read his Bible, or do any of the things that we think good people do. So far as we know, the only *thing* he did was to acknowledge Jesus for who He is. In a verse mentioned earlier, "with the heart one believes unto righteousness." The world saw a criminal dying for his crimes, but God saw righteousness. The same goes for each of us.

It does not matter what the world sees in us. It does not matter what we see in us. At that moment that we believe the Gospel, we are seen as righteous in God's eyes. No other opinion really matters. If God says it's so, it is so. Then with the mouth confession is made unto salvation. This is where the tradition of a "sinner's prayer" comes from. There is no specific formal thing to say. It is just a heartfelt confession of Jesus as Lord. Anyone can do this at any time and any place. And this is truly the first step toward any real progress in life. As can be seen by that guy hanging next to Jesus, it's pretty simple to do, yet it has profound significance.

Once this is done, a great burden is lifted. When this happened to me, I felt like a one-hundred-pound backpack had been taken off of me. I was amazed that my feet still reached the ground because I felt so light. I had no idea of the weight that had been on me. It was a weight of shame and guilt, and it is now gone. Thank You, Jesus.

It's a great deal. There is no downside. There is no financial obligation or commitment to a particular church. There is no quid pro quo. Remember that God so loved that He gave. "For by grace you have been saved through faith, and that not of yourselves; it is the gift of God" (Eph. 2:8). It requires humility on our part to acknowledge that we need it, but beyond that it is just a matter of receiving this gift from God.

"Behold what manner of love the Father has bestowed on us, that we should be called the children of God" (1 John 3:1). Once we believe and accept this wonderful gift, we are in His family. We are welcome in His house. We now have a loving Father who wants to be with us, hear from us, help us, and provide for us. Not everyone has a good example of a father figure. My dad was a wonderful and loving man, a WWII vet who worked hard to provide well for his family. But God is the perfect Father. He is rich beyond comprehension, His love for us knows no bounds, and He is never too busy to drop everything and help us.

That help is the subject of this book. God has not only made the way for us to be in His family, He has given us great tools and resources to achieve great things with the life that He has given us. We want to succeed in life. God also wants us to succeed in life. We're not trying to sneak something past Him. It is His desire that we enjoy a good life. When we get on board and work with Him, there is great power available for the accomplishment of mighty works.

It is not a requirement, but it is a good idea to begin attending regular church services. This provides great opportunities to be mentored and taught, as well as opportunities to serve and to worship. These things will be addressed in this book. Also, in the appendix, is a description of the sacraments of baptism and communion. This will likely come up right away, and I don't want anyone to not know what that's all about.

Read on and be blessed!

Chapter 3

The Word

With any trip or journey, a map is handy. Sometimes it's fun to just go for a drive and see where a road takes us. But if our purpose is to get somewhere specific, a guide to the most direct route will get us there saving time and gas. The Bible is such a guide for the trip of life.

I've heard the acronym used—Basic Instructions Before Leaving Earth. I find it to be the best and easiest way to get to know God, His attitudes, and His values. It is also a great way to see our lives in the context of human existence and to see how an individual can impact the world for good or for bad.

To attribute any credibility to the Bible, we must first come to terms with it being the inspired Word of God. There are many great books that have been published over the years. Some are clearly fiction, some are labeled as nonfiction, but only one is referred to as "The Word of God." It was perhaps easy for me because God spoke to me saying, "Read My Word!" I knew He meant the Bible. He wasn't concerned about any particular translation or where to start, just "Read My Word!"

What is that Word and where did it come from? There are sixty-six books in what we now refer to as the Bible. There are thirty-nine books in the Old Testament and twenty-seven books in the New Testament. For the most part, the Old Testament was originally written in the Hebrew language and the New Testament was written in the Greek language. Although ink was put to paper (or parchment) by the hands of men, God is the author of all of it.

"All scripture is given by inspiration of God, and is profitable for doctrine, for reproof, for correction, for instruction in righteousness" (2 Tim. 3:16). Inspiration through God's Holy Spirit gave the words and people wrote it down. Hebrews 6:18 says, "It is impossible for God to lie." Proverbs 30:5 says, "Every word of God is pure." As the Gospel of John begins, we read, "In the beginning was the Word, and the Word was with God and the Word was God." We can look at the Bible as just another book like *Moby Dick* or *Think and Grow Rich*. But when we read the Bible and see the principles outlined therein, we begin to understand that it is, in fact, truth.

Unless Hebrew and Greek are common languages for us to speak or read, we use what is called a translation. There are many translations available to us today. Some attempt to translate into a more modern English form in a word-for-word manner, while others take a more paraphrased approach. For study purposes, I recommend using several translations and compare them. King James Version (KJV) is good, so is the Amplified Version (AMP). My favorite is the New King James Version (NKJV). Elizabethan English is almost as obsolete a language as Greek in America today. The 1611 King James Version or "Authorized Version" has actually been updated many times since 1611 to make it easier to read. The New King James Version is simply the most recent updated version of the original.

Whatever translation you use, the Holy Spirit is there to help you understand it. (I'll address that in greater detail later in this book.) It is also a very good idea to surround yourself with Bible-believing friends who can help make sure you don't get off track. It is also extremely important to attend a church where the Bible is taught. All people have attitudes, values, opinions, and viewpoints, but God is God and His Word is His Word. Anytime we drift too far from there, we are in jeopardy.

The Bible starts with the Old Testament. The first five books are called the Pentateuch and are attributed to Moses. Then there are a series of historical accounts. The "poetic books" are Job, Psalms, Proverbs, Ecclesiastes, and Song of Solomon. After that are a series of the books of the prophets. There are some that are larger volumes than others, and thus there are what's called the major and minor prophets. It's all God's Word, and it's all good to read and become familiar with the contents.

The New Testament starts with the Gospels—Matthew, Mark, Luke, and John. These are four different accounts of the life and times of Jesus. Matthew and John were actually original disciples of Jesus and traveled with Him during His three-year ministry. All four accounts are God breathed or God inspired and dependable. Even in the secular world, people will say that something is "the Gospel truth" to try to say that something is absolutely true.

After the Gospels, there is the book of Acts, or the Acts of the Apostles, which is a historical book describing events of the early church. After Acts, there are a series of epistles or letters written by Paul, James, Peter, John, and Jude. Paul wrote a large portion of them, and they are all extremely useful in terms of guidance in our travels through our modern-day life. Finally, there is the last book in the Bible, the Revelation of Jesus Christ. This one is a prophetic book, and it details a series of events that will happen in what is known as the *last days* or *end times*.

The Bible altogether is great literature, but it is unique among books. You can read *Tom Sawyer* a hundred times, and it will just get old. Mark Twain was a great author, and this is a great book, but it is just that—a book. The Bible is quite different in that it is alive. I know that is an odd concept. How can something that you don't have to feed or expose to sunlight be alive? You can pack it away somewhere in the dark for years, and then bring it out and read it, and it is fresh and alive. It is something of the Spirit. The books were written by inspiration of God through His Holy Spirit, and His Holy Spirit is with us as we read it. Mark Twain is dead. He cannot sit with us when we read *Tom Sawyer*.

It has been well over twenty-five years since God told me to read His Word. And after reading it many times—some parts, hundreds of times—I still read from it daily. It's like food to me. A person might have a wonderful meal and be very satisfied, but the next day, they'll be hungry again. The Word, or the Bible, is that way also. It isn't something that one studies until they know it all; it's a nourishing experience. Its intimate time spent with God. Not only that, but we can gain deeper and deeper levels of understanding.

Peter says it well. "Grace and peace be multiplied to you in the knowledge of God and of Jesus our Lord, as His divine power has given to us all things that pertain to life and godliness, through the knowledge of Him" (2 Pet. 1:2–3). Peter speaks of grace and peace and all things that pertain to life and godliness and divine power. Wouldn't that be a handy thing to have? It is available through the knowledge of God, which is gained through time spent in His Word.

When we first get saved, we rarely have a clue to the magnitude of what has been given to us. "Oh good," we think. "Now I won't go to hell." That is true, but there is so much more. We have power, we have authority, we have purpose, and we have a hope and a future. Not only does God want to bless us, but through us He wants to bless others. The only way to understand any of that is to read the Bible. At first, we are like baby birds in a nest with our mouths wide open hoping that someone will feed us, but the sooner we learn to feed ourselves, the better off we will be.

When God told me to read His Word, I remembered many stories or expressions that I had heard growing up. Then I began to wonder about them. What's the deal with Jonah and the big fish? How about Noah and the flood, Abraham, Isaac and Jacob, Adam and Eve? I wanted to know. I also wanted to know the context of so many expressions that I had heard over the years. "A little bird told me." "The foxes can spoil the vine." "There are flies in the ointment." "It's not my cross to bear." These are all statements that came from the Bible.

There is no knowledge or understanding in life of greater value than knowledge and understanding of the Word of God. It helps us deal with whatever comes up in life and see it through the overarching truth. God loves us and wants to bless us.

Chapter 4

The Holy Spirit

The term *Holy Trinity* refers to God, the Father, God, the Son, and God the Holy Spirit (or Holy Ghost). The first mention of the Holy Spirit, or *Spirit of God,* is in the second verse of the Bible. "The earth was without form, and void; and darkness was on the face of the deep. And the Spirit of God was hovering over the face of the waters" (Gen. 1:2). The Old Testament has many other references to the Spirit of God.

We read about Jesus, God the Son, in the Gospels. And Jesus speaks often about God the Father, but who is the Holy Spirit? There is a natural or physical realm that we live in where we can see things, hear things, taste things, smell things, and feel things in the world around us. There are also things in what can be referred to as the spiritual realm. These things cannot be experienced or measured physically. For example, if someone is angry, you can't hear or see the anger, only words spoken or facial expressions. The spirit of anger is one thing, and the manifestations of that spirit in the form of a frown or angry words is yet another.

Ice, water, and steam are all the same substance, H_2O, but in different forms. Similarly, God, Jesus, and the Holy Spirit are all one individual yet in three distinct parts. It may be difficult, at first, to comprehend this concept, but don't worry. This Holy Spirit will help us understand. (More on this in a moment.) It is important to gain our understanding from scripture and not just from other people's explanations. Fortunately, the Bible is rich with explanations and examples to teach us. Sadly, for many hundreds of years, most people could not read, and a lot of false teaching developed about this subject.

Some religious traditions have drifted away from the truth of the Word. I feel a little fortunate that I didn't grow up in church and was never exposed to much in the way of religious traditions. I just lumped all that Bible stuff into a religious bucket and ignored it. That is, until I got saved and then God told me to read His Word. I've heard it said, "The person who does not read good books has no advantage over the person who cannot read." I think that is an excellent expression. We can read, and we should read. Oh, how foolish to ignore the greatest resource book ever written—the Bible.

In John's Gospel, we read some wonderful things that Jesus said to His disciples in an upper room the night that He was betrayed. In several verses, Jesus speaks about the Holy Spirit. He refers to Him as the Helper or the Spirit of Truth. "And I will pray the Father, and He will give you another Helper, that He may abide with you forever, the Spirit of truth, whom the world cannot receive, because it neither sees Him nor knows Him; but you know Him, for He dwells with you and will be in you" (John 14:16–17).

"These things I have spoken to you while being present with you. But the Helper, the Holy Spirit, whom the Father will send in My name, He will teach you all things, and bring to your remembrance all things that I said to you" (John 14:25–26). "However, when He, the Spirit of truth, has come, He will guide you into all truth, for He will not speak on His own authority, but whatever He hears He will speak; and He will tell you things to come. He will glorify Me, for He will take of what is Mine and declare it to you. All things that the Father has are Mine. Therefore, I said that He will take of Mine and declare it to you" (John 16:13–15).

The opportunity is there to think that Jesus was saying these things only to the disciples that were in the room with Him at that time. But Jesus goes on to clarify that this was meant for us also, as believers: "I do not pray for these alone, but also for those who will believe in Me through their word" (John 17:20). None of the blessings, commands, or promises that Jesus spoke of were just for a generation of people who all died almost two thousand years ago. They are for all believers since then—including us!

At the end of Luke's Gospel, Jesus says, "Behold, I send the Promise of My Father upon you; but tarry in the city of Jerusalem until you are endued with power from on high" (Luke 24:49). Many years before the birth of Jesus, a time was spoken of by the prophet Joel. "And it shall come to pass afterward that I will pour out My Spirit on all flesh" (Joel 2:28). This began on the day of Pentecost, which is described in detail in Acts chapter two.

"But you shall receive power when the Holy Spirit has come upon you; and you shall be witnesses to Me in Jerusalem, and in all Judea and Samaria, and to the end of the earth" (Acts 1:8). Jesus spoke these words right before He ascended into heaven. Then in the next chapter, we read about what many consider to be the birth of the New Testament church. Pentecost was a Jewish holiday, and 120 disciples were gathered in an upper room in Jerusalem when the fulfillments of Joel's prophesy began. "And they were all filled with the Holy Spirit and began to speak with other tongues, as the Spirit gave them utterance" (Acts 2:4).

I'm not making this up. Please read the Bible for yourself. Base your faith on the truth of the Word and not just in anything that some person says. The Word is the standard for truth. It may seem strange that God could just speak words so that things were created. It may seem strange that Jesus could just speak words and people were healed. It may seem strange that God loves us. But if the Bible says it is so, it is so, and that is what I believe—no matter what anybody else says. God has more credibility with me than any person.

These people in that upper room were believers in Jesus. They were born again believers and had been for several days. But on this day, they were filled with the Holy Spirit. This tells us that a person can be saved, born again, part of the family of God, going to heaven when they die, but not filled with the Holy Spirit. When a person accepts Jesus as Lord and believes the Gospel, he is saved, but this being filled with the Holy Spirit is a separate and distinct other event. (Although they can both happen at the same time.) As we read on through the book of Acts, we see many other examples of believers who later were filled with the Holy Spirit (Acts 8:14–17; 9:17; 10:44–46; 11:15; 15:8; 18:24–26; 19:2–6).

I have heard many times from preachers (some of whom I have great respect for otherwise) say, "When a person is born again, they receive a portion of the Holy Spirit and that is it. There is no subsequent filling of the Holy Spirit." That is just not true, according to the Bible. Some things are subject to a person's interpretation, but here we have eight examples from scripture to establish a truth. "By the mouth of two or three witnesses every word shall be established" (2 Cor. 13:1 and Deut. 17:6).

For a long time, I wondered just where the notion came from that something has changed, and these promises were no longer in effect. Then I finally heard someone give what they thought was a scriptural basis for not believing in being filled with the Holy Spirit today. They quoted 1 Corinthians 13, "But whether there are prophecies, they will fail; whether there are tongues, they will cease; whether there is knowledge, it will vanish away" (1 Cor. 13:8). Okay, there is a mention of tongues ceasing, but in the broader context of that passage, it says that prophesies will fail and knowledge will vanish. Paul was describing an event that has not yet occurred. "But when that which is perfect has come, that which is in part will be done away" (1 Cor. 13:10). "For now we see in a mirror, dimly, but then face to face. Now I know in part, but then I shall know just as I also am known" (1 Cor. 13:12). We are still in the *now*; the *then* will happen when we go to be with the Lord, or when He comes back to the earth.

This speaking in other tongues that appears to be part of this being filled with the Holy Spirit is a challenging thing to accept. On the Day of Pentecost mentioned earlier, those people in that upper room were all speaking in other tongues. These other tongues were in large part languages that they didn't know or had never learned. The Holy Spirit was giving them utterance. People nearby who heard them were visiting Jerusalem from other lands since Pentecost was an established holiday when people would go to Jerusalem to worship. These people marveled that those disciples spoke in their language about the wonderful works of God. Evidently there was a lot of laughter and commotion in that upper room also. As Peter began to address the crowd about what was going on, the first thing he said was that they were not drunk.

Paul says this, "I wish you all spoke with tongues, but even more that you prophesied" (1 Cor. 14:5). This speaking in tongues is a way for our spirit to pray without our brains needing to be involved. Often, I want to pray about something, but I don't know enough about the situation to verbalize my concern. "Likewise the Spirit also helps in our weakness. For we do not know what we should pray for as we ought, but the Spirit Himself makes intercession for us with groanings which cannot be uttered" (Rom. 8:26).

The human language is so limiting at times. Praying in the Spirit, as this is called, is a way for us to speak with God spirit to Spirit. Also, sometimes we just don't know the words to properly declare just how much we love God and how we want to thank Him for all He does. How can words describe the beauty of Jesus? Why limit our ability to express our love by our vocabulary? There are many gifts of the Holy Spirit detailed in 1 Corinthians. I just want it known that this Holy Spirit is available.

As I mentioned earlier, Jesus said, "But the Helper, the Holy Spirit, whom the Father will send in My name, He will teach you all things, and bring to remembrance all things that I said to you" (John 14:26). This is another wonderful benefit to being filled with the Holy Spirit. Whenever I read the Bible, He's there with me to help me understand. He also helps me recall other verses of scripture that relate to what I'm reading. The Bible really comes alive when He's there with me as a guide.

From Luke 24:49 and Acts 1:8, Jesus says we will be endued with power or receive power. This is the power needed to accomplish things for God. There is only so much any of us can do in our own strength. But the things done by the early church leaders were done through the power of the Holy Spirit. When a great man does great things, he is glorified. But when an ordinary man does extraordinary things, God is glorified.

I could go on and on about times when the Holy Spirit cautioned me while driving, or told me to give someone money, or caused me to hold back words that could have been destructive. He is a Helper indeed! Don't be frightened by labels that people give. Churches can be labeled "Pentecostal" or "Charismatic." People can be labeled as a "holy roller." It doesn't matter. To have the power to do the things that God has called us to do, we need the Holy Spirit.

Chapter 5

Spirit, Soul, and Body

Now that we've gained a little understanding of the nature of God, we should understand a little about the nature of people. We are probably all aware of the fact that we are, as people, more than just our bodies. Just about every civilization has acknowledged a nonphysical component that endures beyond the death of the body.

We are all very much aware of our bodies, but we are spirits who dwell in these bodies. There will come a time when this body ceases to function—it will die, but we will continue to exist. Paul refers to the body as "This earthly house, this tent" (2 Cor. 5:1). Our bodies are necessary tools for us to live our earthly lives in, and we should respect and take care of them. But we are so much more than that.

I remember a scene in a movie where Charlton Hesston was playing the role of John the Baptist. In the movie, King Herod had imprisoned John the Baptist and was about to execute him. Herod asked, "Do you know why I am here?" To which John replied, "To release me." Herod said, "No. I'm here to kill you." John's reply was, "Ah, then you release me!" (Charlton Hesston delivered that line so well that it left quite an impression on me.) In that scene, John the Baptist saw death as a release from his earthly situation. That was just a movie, of course, but it illustrates this point rather well.

First of all, when we get born again—when we believed the Gospel—our spirits are what is reborn. Jesus had a conversation with a man named Nicodemus who was a Pharisee and a ruler of the Jews.

Jesus said, "Unless one is born again, he cannot see the kingdom of God" (John 3:3). This was difficult for Nicodemus to understand. Jesus went on to explain, "I say to you, unless one is born of water and the Spirit, he cannot enter the kingdom of God. That which is born of the flesh is flesh, and that which is born of the Spirit is spirit. Do not marvel that I said to you, 'You must be born again.' The wind blows where it wishes, and you hear the sound of it but cannot tell where it comes from and where it goes. So is everyone who is born of the Spirit" (John 3:5–8).

"But he who is joined to the Lord is one spirit with Him" (1 Cor. 6:17). "But God, who is rich in mercy, because of His great love with which He loved us, even when we were dead in trespasses, made us alive together with Christ (by grace you have been saved), and raised us up together, and made us sit together in the heavenly places in Christ Jesus" (Eph. 2:4–7). That may all seem a little abstract right now but understand this—at that moment when we believed, our spirit was reborn, our spirit was made perfect and in union with God.

Our bodies don't instantly change when we receive Jesus as Lord. Don't expect to immediately gain or lose weight. Tattoos don't disappear; we don't change our physical appearance, other than perhaps a big smile. Our bodies are often referred to as our *flesh*. When we turn the crank on a jack-in-the-box, and the clown pops out, we might flinch. This is not because we are truly afraid of that little clown. Our body, our flesh, simply reacts on its own. This is something to be aware of. We are a new person, and new values and attitudes are developing in our mind. But our flesh will still respond to the same stimuli that it always responded to in the past. This may be the smell of a pizza or the sight of a pretty girl, but our flesh is subject to earthly stimulation.

There is something also that is called the *soul*. "Now may the God of peace Himself sanctify you completely; and may your whole spirit, soul, and body be preserved blameless at the coming of our Lord Jesus Christ" (1 Thess. 5:23). The soul is traditionally referred to as our mind, will, and emotions. A lot of our individual personality comes from our mind, will, and emotions. We are spirit beings, we have a soul, and we live, for now, in a body. This may be a challenge to comprehend at first, not unlike God existing as the Father, the Son, and the Holy Spirit. But when we gain this understanding, much of what we read in the Bible will make a lot more sense.

"For the word of God is living and powerful and sharper than any two-edged sword, piercing even to the division of soul and spirit, and of joints and marrow, and is a discerner of the thoughts and intents of the heart" (Heb. 4:12). Our spirit and our soul are our nonphysical components, but they are distinct from one another. Our thoughts, our feelings, and our intentions can change. As a matter of fact, this is the essence of what can be called "maturing as a Christian." Just as an athlete or a musician disciplines his body to perform, we develop the discipline to govern our thoughts and feelings. And this is a lifelong process.

"I say then: walk in the Spirit and you shall not fulfill the lust of the flesh. For the flesh lusts against the Spirit, and the Spirit against the flesh; and these are contrary to one another, so that you do not do the things that you wish" (Gal. 5:16–17). In the secular world, the term *lust of the flesh* conjures up all sorts of images, but it might simply be something like wanting to say something unkind to someone who just hurt us, and not necessarily have anything to do with rape or murder.

Paul goes on to explain, "Now the works of the flesh are evident, which are: adultery, fornication, uncleanness, lewdness, idolatry, sorcery, hatred, contentions, jealousies, outbursts of wrath, selfish ambitions, dissensions, heresies, envy, murders, drunkenness, revelries, and the like" (Gal. 5:19–21). This does not mean that if we do one of these things that we are going to hell. This is just a list of what our flesh, on its own, naturally wants to do. This is what we should be on guard of. When we catch ourselves wanting to do these things, just stop.

It's not simply a matter of doing these things but thinking about or talking about these things as well. "There is therefore now no condemnation to those who are in Christ Jesus, who do not walk according to the flesh, but according to the Spirit" (Rom. 8:1). "For those who live according to the flesh set their minds on the things of the flesh, but those who live according to the Spirit, the things of the Spirit. For to be carnally minded is death, but to be spiritually minded is life and peace" (Rom. 8:5–6). Did you notice the expression *set their minds on*? We choose what we set our minds on. Paul uses the term *carnally minded*. This simply means to be thinking solely of the natural, physical realm, whereas to be *spiritually minded* is to be thinking of things in the spirit realm.

What are the things of the Spirit realm? Paul describes that this way: "But the fruit of the Spirit is love, joy, peace, long-suffering (or patience), kindness, goodness, faithfulness, gentleness, and self-control" (Gal. 5:22–23). What are our thoughts when we see things going on around us? Are we judging or comparing people according to natural standards? As we mature and become more spiritually minded, our thoughts, emotions, and motives become driven more by love and empathy than envy or some other negative emotion.

I've heard the expression, "He's so spiritually minded that he's no earthly good." That is a carnal perspective. I would rather that be said of me than that I was "So naturally minded that I am of no spiritual good." Paul says it well here, "Rejoice in the Lord always. Again I will say, rejoice! Let your gentleness be known to all men. The Lord is at hand. Be anxious for nothing, but in everything by prayer and supplication, with thanksgiving, let your requests be made known to God; and the peace of God, which surpasses all understanding, will guard your hearts and minds through Christ Jesus" (Phil. 4:4–7).

Back to the idea of setting our minds on things, Paul tells us this, "Finally, brethren, whatever things are true, whatever things are noble, whatever things are just, whatever things are pure, whatever things are lovely, whatever things are of good report, if there is any virtue and if there is anything praiseworthy, meditate on these things" (Phil. 4:8).

Our minds are like a garden, and what grows there has a lot to do with how we tend our garden. "Do not be deceived, God is not mocked; for whatever a man sows, that he will also reap. For he who sows to his flesh will of the flesh reap corruption, but he who sows to the Spirit will of the Spirit reap everlasting life" (Gal. 6:7–8). Be the gardener who takes good care of his garden. Pull the weeds, plant and water the right crops. Each of us are responsible for our own thoughts. Each of us are responsible for what grows from our lives. This book is designed to be a help, but the Bible is the key. Spend time in the Word routinely. Develop an appetite for the Word. Surround yourself with people who will help you mature in the Lord.

CHAPTER 6

About Covenants

In business, many deals or transactions are made. Often these are simple and relatively inconsequential deals. I might give the person at the counter a dollar, and they give me a cup of coffee. Other things are much more complicated and need to be spelled out, item by item with a formal contract.

In the Bible, we read about *covenants*. A covenant is more than just an agreement. It is a solemn contract, an oath between two parties. A covenant is a framework for a relationship. That is why marriage is considered a covenant. God has made several covenants with people. The first one mentioned in the Bible was between God and Noah. "But I will establish My covenant with you; and you shall go into the ark—you and your sons, your wife, and your sons' wives with you" (Gen. 6:18). Later, in Genesis 9, God explains some details of this covenant. This covenant was between God and Noah, plus every living creature, that He would never again destroy all flesh. (Like He did with the flood.) To signify this covenant, He created the rainbow as a sign.

Then God made a covenant with Abram, promising Abram all the land that later became Israel. This would become known as the Promised Land. God had Abram cut several animals in two and laid them out on the ground. A deep sleep came over Abram, and then a smoking oven and a burning torch passed between the pieces. Abram was ninety-nine years old and childless. God told him that He would make him a father of many nations and make him exceedingly fruitful, and from then on, he would be called Abraham. For a sign of this covenant, God gave the command for circumcision. This was the great covenant that was spoken of up until the Israelites came out of Egypt. This was about the nation of Israel and the land promised to them.

Another covenant was made—this time with Moses. This one is called the covenant of the law, or in the New Testament, it is referred to as the Old Covenant. Now there's documentation. God wrote the Ten Commandments on stone tablets. God also spoke in great detail about many other things. Much of Exodus from chapter nineteen on and most of Leviticus and Deuteronomy detail the law as God gave it to Moses. There were over six hundred laws. There were regulations and specific ways that the tabernacle was to be fashioned and how to conduct religious services and who was to do what. There were specific forms of punishment described for any laws broken, including the death penalty. The general term for any transgression or failure to abide by any provision of the law is *sin*.

As it turns out, nobody was able to live a life without breaking at least one of those laws. I mean absolutely nobody except Jesus, but I'll get to that in a moment. The Old Covenant was a performance-based covenant. "Now it shall come to pass that if you diligently obey the voice of the Lord your God, to observe carefully all the commandments which I command you today, that the Lord your God will set you high above all nations of the earth. And all these blessings shall come upon you and overtake you, because you obey the voice of the Lord your God" (Deut. 28:1–2). Note the condition—if you observe carefully all the commandments. What follows is a list of very nice blessings.

"But it shall come to pass, if you do not obey the voice of the Lord your God, to observe carefully all His commandments and His statutes which I command you today, that all these curses will come upon you and overtake you" (Deut. 28:15). What follows is a long list of very bad curses. Note again the performance-based nature of this. And it's all or nothing. "For whoever shall keep the whole law, and yet stumble in one point, he shall be guilty of all" (James 2:10).

This is known as the curse of the law, and all are guilty. "For all have sinned and fall short of the glory of God" (Rom. 3:23). Why would God make a deal with mankind that would doom everyone to hell? "I would not have known sin except through the law" (Rom. 7:7). All that law accomplished one thing—it let everyone know that they were utterly hopeless on their own.

Then came Jesus. John the Baptist said, "Behold the lamb of God who takes away the sin of the world" (John 1:29). There were blood sacrifices described in the law that would atone for people's sins for each time they were committed. And it was Jesus' purpose to be the ultimate sacrifice for all the sin of mankind for all time. That is why, when Jesus was born, the angels sang, "Glory to God in the Highest, and on earth peace, goodwill toward men!" (Luke 2:14). There wasn't peace between God and man because of sin. Jesus came to make that peace. His blood ratified a New Covenant, a covenant of grace.

"For God so loved the world that He gave His only begotten Son that whosoever believes in Him shall not perish but have everlasting life" (John 3:16). Jesus said, "Do not think that I came to destroy the law or the prophets. I did not come to destroy but to fulfill" (Matt. 5:17). "For the wages of sin is death, but the gift of God is eternal life in Christ Jesus our Lord" (Rom. 6:23). "But God demonstrates His own love toward us, in that while we were still sinners, Christ died for us" (Rom. 5:8). "For whoever calls on the name of the Lord shall be saved" (Rom. 10:13).

"For if that first covenant (the law) had been faultless, then no place would have been sought for a second" (Heb. 8:7). "He says, *a new covenant*. He has made the first obsolete. Now what is becoming obsolete and growing old is ready to vanish away" (Heb. 8:13). "How much more shall the blood of Christ, who through the eternal Spirit offered Himself without spot to God, cleanse your conscience from dead works to serve the living God" (Heb. 8:14). "But this Man, after He had offered one sacrifice for sins forever, sat down at the right hand of God" (Heb. 10:12). "By that will we have been sanctified through the offering of the body of Jesus Christ once for all" (Heb. 10:10).

There we have it—a New Covenant that replaces the old one. A New Covenant ratified by the blood of Jesus, whose death on the cross paid for the sin of mankind once and for all. That means all of it—past, present, and future—for everybody. Nobody is excluded. No particular sin is excluded. That seems like a lot, but several times the Bible describes the sacrifice of Jesus as *much more* than what was needed. It's like giving someone a million-dollar bill to cover a ninety-eight-cent bill and saying, "Keep the change." What He paid was much more because of who He is. It is mind-boggling to think that God loves us that much, but He does.

This New Covenant is often referred to as the Covenant of Grace—as opposed to the Covenant of the Law. Grace is traditionally defined as the unmerited, undeserved, unearned favor of God. "It is a gift of God, not of works, lest anyone should boast" (Eph. 2:8–9). If a friend asked me over for dinner just for us to spend some time together, that would be like *grace*. He would not expect payment or even a tip. The meal is a gift, and it is already paid for, and he just wanted to bless me. Grace, in the context of Ephesians 2:8, is a much greater gift. It is the favor of God. That is so much more than marrying the boss's daughter or being the mayor's neighbor.

This is a covenant, though, and not just an entitlement. It's not automatic for anybody. There is something that everybody must do, and that is to receive it by faith. "For by grace you have been saved through faith, and that not of yourselves; it is a gift of God" (Eph. 2:8). It is a gift. Grace is the undeserved, unmerited favor of God. But it is only received through faith in Jesus Christ. This is harder than it might seem at first. It requires the humility to confess that we are absolutely helpless without that grace. It also requires that we believe it.

It's not enough to just believe in God. "You believe that there is one God. You do well. Even the demons believe and tremble" (James 2:19). We must receive it by faith. A truck may back up to our dock, but we have to open the door and receive the freight. This freight we receive by faith in Jesus. All that means is that we acknowledge Who He is and what He has done for us. "For with the heart one believes unto righteousness, and with the mouth confession is made unto salvation" (Rom. 10:10).

Absolutely no one has anything to boast about. This great gift is not something we can earn. But it is something that God paid dearly for, and He wants us all to have it. We are part of the New Covenant because we believe in Jesus and confess Him as Lord. The blessings are ours because of Jesus, His obedience, and the grace of God. Nothing that we do or don't do is a factor other than believing and confessing—that is to receive the gift.

This is not to say that our behavior has no consequence. Lying, cheating, stealing, and so on, all have consequences. Our own conscience will nag us when we do things that we know we shouldn't. Hatred, unforgiveness, envy—all have an impact on how well our faith will work. But by no means is our salvation contingent upon good behavior. All through the Bible, especially in the Proverbs, God shows us how to be fruitful and lead a satisfying life. Bad behavior or sin can only hinder that.

The Old Covenant was based on a man's performance and how good he was. The New Covenant is based on Jesus and how good He is. A person might be the vilest, most evil fool that ever was, but when he comes to Jesus, all is forgiven, and he is welcomed into the family. None of us have any reason to think we are any better than that. The law describes the purity and high standards of God, and He has not changed nor will He ever. But our relationship with Him has changed. The Ten Commandments are posted in front of the old courthouse in the small town where I live. They are still valid. You should not do the "thou shalt nots," and you should do all the "thou shalts." This is living right. But your salvation is by the grace of God through your faith in Jesus Christ.

Chapter 7

Benefits

It may seem a little crass or tacky to speak of *benefits* in a relationship, as if I was asking, "What's in it for me?" But I get this term right from the Bible. In a moment, we will read a verse from Psalm 103 to clarify this point. There are some distinct advantages to being a Christian. It's always good to know what we can count on.

This Covenant of Grace that we spoke of in the last chapter has some specific provisions that we, as believers, can claim. Remember, if it is grace, it is not contingent upon our behavior. We must simply receive it. But before we can receive anything, we must know, without doubt, that it is ours to receive. That is why it is so important to base our beliefs on the Word of God.

There have been times when I was working for a company that had employment benefits. The human resources department would publish a brochure that listed the specific benefits that were offered. These would be benefits like health insurance, paid time off, a 401K, or something offered by the employer as an incentive to keep me working for them. Many times I would have to ask for it or enroll in some program, but these were benefits that I was entitled to. When we find a promise in the Bible, it's ours to claim. How do we go to HR and make our claim? Just like receiving salvation, we simply go to the Father, declare the need, and ask for it.

Psalms 103:1–5 says this, "Bless the Lord, oh my soul; and all that is within me, bless His holy name! Bless the Lord, oh my soul, and forget not all His benefits; Who forgives all your iniquities; Who heals all your diseases; Who redeems your life from destruction; Who crowns you with loving kindness and tender mercies; Who satisfies your mouth with good things, so that your youth is renewed like an eagle's."

Note the reaction of the writer of this psalm. When he realized these benefits, his heart was filled with gratitude. It should be the same way for us. There is no greater benefits package offered by anyone ever. Hallelujah! Thank You, Lord, for your wonderful grace. Remember that we don't work to receive anything; this is given to us as part of the New Covenant. This is part of the framework for our relationship with God.

He forgives all our iniquities. There is a wage for sin. That wage is death. And that wage was paid by Jesus Himself. He took upon Himself the sin of the world. His blood sacrifice paid for and brought atonement once and for all to all who will believe in Him. On the cross, He said, "It is finished." The whole matter of sin is a done thing for believers, and we should not live in fear of hell or damnation ever again. We now have the Righteousness of Christ.

Then the Psalmist says that He heals all our diseases. Amazing! Jesus took upon Himself all our diseases, along with the sin of the world, when He went to that cross. That's supposed to be finished also. In Isaiah 53: 5, the prophet says that "by His stripes we are healed." Peter reaffirms that in 1 Peter 2:24. This isn't some metaphor about sins. This means exactly what it says. By the stripes, the wounds of abuse and crucifixion, of Jesus, we are healed of diseases. The punishment (the whipping) He received on our behalf brought about physical healing for us.

He redeems our life from destruction. It doesn't matter how many mistakes we've made, how many bad decisions, how many wrong turns. He can turn things around and make things good. I have known many people who had gone a long way down a path that leads to destruction. People who have lost jobs, homes, wives, children, who thought they had lost it all (I was such a person), who have had it all restored to them by God. It doesn't matter if a person is in a hospital, in jail or prison, homeless, broke, or whatever—God is ready to turn things around.

He crowns us with lovingkindness and tender mercies. Many people think that God is mad at them and is ready to give them a spanking. But when the prodigal son returned, his father ran to meet him (see Luke 15:11–32). Likewise, our Father is running to meet us with open arms. He loves us and wants to shower us with tender mercies. This is His nature. This may not be what we think we deserve, but that doesn't matter. What matters is His love for us and what He wants to do, which is to welcome us into the family.

He satisfies our mouths with good things. God "gives richly all things to enjoy" (1 Tim. 6:17). We can learn a lot about how God wants to treat us by what He did with Adam and Eve at the very beginning. In the first chapter of Genesis, we read about God creating a paradise in the form of a garden where everything was beautiful, abundant, and provided free. As soon as God created man, He blessed him. "Then God blessed them and said to them, 'Be fruitful and multiply'" (Gen. 1:29). These were the first words spoken by God to man—the first commandment from God. Likewise, God wants to bless us and provide whatever is needed for us to be fruitful.

In Matthew 6, Jesus tells us not to worry about things like what we will wear and what we will eat. He used the flowers of the field and the birds to illustrate how God provides everything needed. We don't just sit by the pool and wait for checks to come in the mail, but we seek first the kingdom of God, and those things are added to us (Matt. 6:33). Or as Peter puts it, "His divine power has given to us all things that pertain to life and godliness, through the knowledge of Him who called us by glory and virtue" (2 Pet. 1:3).

Our youth is renewed like an eagle. The older I get, the more exciting this sounds. Moses was eighty years old when he began his great work. Abraham was a hundred years old when he began having children. Noah was over four hundred years old when he began building the ark. The world says that when we get older, we become feeble and useless. This is a lie! Don't accept it. We should never put upon ourselves a mantle of dissipation. As long as we are willing, God will make us able to have an impact. Every morning, I declare that I will enjoy the perfect health, joy, and peace that Jesus bought for me at Calvary. There is great power in making a declaration like that, and I will explain that in more detail later in this book.

The benefits package includes much more than just the five or six items mentioned in Psalm 103. We will spend a lifetime discovering the wonderful gifts from God. This is just part of why it is good to read the Word daily. Aside from the spiritual nourishment and the time spent alone with God, we find things that apply to our current situations. Whenever we read about how He has blessed someone, we can ask for that blessing for ourselves. It's as if we are applying to HR for an employment benefit. Not everything happens immediately, but if it is a promise from God, it is a sure thing. We must just stand in faith and receive it. We'll talk more about faith in a later chapter. We have specific benefits associated with our covenant with God.

Chapter 8

Understanding Grace

If someone came up to me and said, "Hey, John, will you sing me a song for a hundred dollars?" I'd sing that man a song. If he then gave me $100 that would be considered a wage for work done. If someone just came up to me and said, "Here's a hundred dollars. I just want you to have it. It's a gift." That would be grace.

Traditionally, grace has been known as the undeserved, unmerited, unearned favor of God. "For it is by grace (God's unmerited favor) that you are saved (delivered from judgment and made partakers of Christ's salvation) through [your] faith. And this [salvation] is not of yourselves [of your own doing, it came not through your own striving], but it is the gift of God" (Eph. 2:8 AMP).

I've heard it put this way, "Mercy is not receiving what we deserve, and grace is receiving what we do not deserve." Wages are earned. If we work for it, it is a wage. Grace is simply given. If we work for that, it then becomes a wage. And when it comes to salvation, nobody can work that hard or that long. The blessings of God offered through the gift of His grace are so great that they can only be received as a gift. It may be that some person may be so rich that they could buy the Taj Mahal. But nobody has enough money or credit to buy the Milky Way galaxy.

When I first began my new life as a Christian, I was confused about this issue. "For God so loved the world that He gave His only begotten Son that whosoever believed in Him shall not perish but have everlasting life" (John 3:16). I believed thus I was saved. But it seemed that there was a lot of emphasis put on my behaviors by the church community. On one hand it was, "Believe the Gospel." And then on the other hand it was, "Don't dare sin." Some sins were easy to deal with—don't murder, don't steal, don't lie, don't commit adultery. But others were much more of a challenge. "But I say to you that whoever looks at a woman to lust for her has already committed adultery with her in his heart" (Matt. 5:28). And "But I say to you that whosoever is angry with his brother without a cause shall be in danger of the judgment" (Matt. 5:22).

I was familiar with the Ten Commandments. That was tough enough, but I had also read through Leviticus and knew there were a lot more laws than just the ten. Breaking any law was *sin*, and I was guilty. Everyone at church put on a pretty good front. I wondered how I was going to make it. Then I gained an understanding of the grace of God. People don't gain favor with God because they behave nicely. They behave nicely because they have gained favor with God.

The moment I realized what Jesus paid for that was given to me, I simply wanted to show gratitude by honoring Him with the way I lived. I no longer thought of sin as something that would damn me to hell but something that would not glorify God. I wanted my life to be a good witness to the world about God's goodness. I used to be known as a guy who knew a lot of dirty jokes, or that I could roll a really good joint. I now would rather be known as someone kind and generous—a good representation of Jesus.

Paul says, "Stand fast therefore in the liberty by which Christ has made us free, and do not be entangled again with a yoke of bondage" (Gal. 5:1). That *yoke* he referred to was the Old Covenant law. He goes on to say, "You have become estranged from Christ, you who attempt to be justified by the law; you have fallen from grace" (Gal. 5:4). "But that no one is justified by the law in the sight of God" (Gal. 3:11). "For by grace you have been saved through faith, and that not of yourselves; it is the gift of God, not by works, lest anyone should boast" (Eph. 2:8–9).

There was a challenging passage in the book of Hebrews, "For if we sin willfully after we have received the knowledge of the truth, there no longer remains a sacrifice for sins" (Heb. 10:26). This does not mean that if I intentionally state something incorrect on a tax return or consumer survey that there now is no hope for me. James says this, "For whoever shall keep the whole law, and yet stumble in one point, he is guilty of all" (James 2:10). Forgiveness of sin, once and for all, was given to me the very moment I believed. "By that will we have been sanctified through the offering of the body of Jesus Christ once for all" (Heb. 10:10).

"Of how much worse punishment, do you suppose will he be thought worthy who has trampled the Son of God underfoot, counted the blood of the covenant by which he was sanctified a common thing and insulted the Spirit of grace" (Heb. 10:29). Like what Paul said in Galatians about having "fallen from grace," when we look to the law for our justification, we are ignoring what Jesus did for us on the cross. Insulting the Spirit of grace is to look at ourselves and to what we do or don't do, instead of looking to Jesus and what He did for us.

Jesus said, "It is finished," when He died on the cross (John 19:30). What He was referring to was ratifying, with His blood, a New Covenant between God and man. "Do not think that I came to destroy the Law or the Prophets. I did not come to destroy but to fulfill" (Matt. 5:17). All the righteous requirements of the law were satisfied by what He did. We, as believers, are justified by grace. "For the wages of sin is death, but the gift of God is eternal life in Christ Jesus, our Lord" (Rom. 6:23).

We recently had some work done on the roof of our home. Some of the guys that did the work were taller than some of the others, but they all got up on the roof by a ladder. Nobody was so tall that they could just step up onto the roof without the ladder. God's standard is perfection. Nobody ever has or ever could achieve that but through Jesus. He is the perfect One. And He shed His blood to restore all mankind to the relationship with God, like He had with Adam at the beginning. This gift was offered once and for all on the cross at Calvary. The gift is grace, and we receive it by faith when we believe.

I will explain about faith in the next chapter. But don't think that this is work to be accomplished. Remember that the grace of God is a gift freely given to all who believe. Our response is simply to love Him and say thank you. We say thank you in many ways. We also care about the things that God cares about, like people. Carrying this great gift of grace with us makes us want to share it with others. I will talk more about that in a later chapter also.

Chapter 9

Understanding Faith

In the previous chapter, I spoke about someone giving me a $100 bill. The offering of that gift would be grace. Faith would be when I receive that $100 bill. I would take hold of it with my hand, fold it up, and put it in my pocket and say, "It is mine." It's not enough to simply acknowledge the gift or be aware of its existence. I must take possession of it. That is faith.

I might be discouraged about something, and someone would say, "God loves you. It's going to be all right." At that point, I could say, "Oh, I hope so." That would be hoping. There's not much power in that. But if I stop and think about it and then say, "I receive that." At that point, I begin assuming that it will, in fact, be all right. My mood changes, and I begin looking for the signs of a turnaround in the situation. That is faith.

Hebrews 11 speaks a lot about faith. It begins with this, "Now faith is the substance of things hoped for, the evidence of things not seen." Hoping for something is one thing, but when we believe it in faith, it then has substance. When that source of inspiration is a verse or passage of scripture, my faith becomes very strong because it is based on truth. A verse that helps me with this is, "Every word of God is pure. He is a shield to those who put their trust in Him" (Prov. 30:5). This verse reminds me about the truth of the Word and the fact that, when I trust God, He becomes a shield for me. I become shielded from doubts and discouragement.

God has said some amazing things. "Then God said, 'Let there be light,' and there was light" (Gen. 1:3). One might think that some wireless device could accomplish this, but this was on the first day of creation. He had not yet created the sun, the moon, any stars, or any other natural, or even artificial, sources for light. He said it and boom! There was light. It's as if light had no option but to obey, even if it was not possible through any natural means. We might think someone is creative if they paint, sculpt, or play music. But God is, to say the least, very creative. Paul puts it this way, "God, who gives life to the dead and calls those things which do not exist as though they did" (Rom. 4:17). "By faith we understand that the worlds were formed by the word of God, so that the things which are seen were not made of things which are visible" (Heb. 11:3).

In that fourth chapter of Romans, Paul talks about Abraham. Abraham and his wife, Sarah, were very old by modern standards. They were both well past the usual child-bearing age. God had told Abraham that he would have a large family. "I will make you a great nation" (Gen. 12:2). Abraham, despite evidence to the contrary, believed God. "And he believed in the Lord, and He accounted it to him for righteousness" (Gen. 15:6). Abraham was around one hundred years old, and Sarah was in her nineties and still childless, but Abraham believed God.

I like to think of faith as having two components. The first component is believing that God *can* do something. "And being fully convinced that what He had promised He was able to perform" (Rom. 4:21). This verse was about Abraham believing God even though his natural circumstances didn't look promising. Abraham was *fully convinced* that God was *able* to do what He had promised.

Once we believe that God *can* do something, the other component is believing that He *will* do what He promised. "By faith Sarah herself also received strength to conceive seed, and she bore a child when she was past the age, because she judged Him faithful who had promised" (Heb. 11:11). This represents what I call the recipe for faith. Has God promised me something? Can He do that? And is He faithful to follow up on a promise? When my answers are yes, yes, and yes, I have faith.

ARE WE THERE YET?

An Old Testament prophet said this, "God is not a man that He should lie, or the son of man, that He should repent. Has He said and will He not do? Or has He spoken, and will He not make it good?" (Num. 23:19). My personal belief is that, if God said it, He will do it. And if He has spoken, He will make it good. We must each develop our own confidence in God's Word. It's a personal thing between each of us and God. His promises are to us as individuals. "But without faith it is impossible to please Him, for he who comes to God must believe that He is, and that He is a rewarder of those who diligently seek Him" (Heb. 11:6).

Our salvation hinges on this. "By grace you have been saved through faith" (Eph. 2:8). "With the heart one believes unto righteousness" (Rom. 10:10). We've heard the Gospel, believed it, and received Jesus as our Savior. And even though we don't get a membership card in the mail, we know that we now are in the family of God. "Behold what manner of love the Father has bestowed on us, that we should be called children of God" (1 John 3:1). We won't see all the evidence until we are in heaven, but we take it on faith that we will someday.

There are many other promises that God has made that relate to more tangible things of this lifetime. "Grace and peace be multiplied to you in the knowledge of God and of Jesus our Lord, as His divine power has given to us all things that pertain to life and godliness, through the knowledge of Him who called us by glory and virtue, by which have been given to us exceedingly great and precious promises" (2 Pet. 1:2–4). "For if by the one man's offense (Adam's) death reigned through the one, much more those who receive abundance of grace and of the gift of righteousness will reign in life through the One, Jesus Christ" (Rom. 5:17). Take this from that verse—the abundance of grace is *much more* than that of sin and death. Our righteousness is a *gift*. And we are to reign *in life* through Jesus.

"And suddenly, a woman who had a flow of blood for twelve years came from behind and touched the hem of His garment. For she said to herself, 'If only I may touch His garment, I shall be made well.' But Jesus turned around and said, 'Be of good cheer, daughter; your faith has made you well.' And the woman was made well from that hour" (Matt. 9:20–22). She had heard about the healing power of Jesus and wanted it for herself. She didn't just hope for it, but she took action. She made her way through a crowd and, on her hands and knees, grabbed hold of His clothes to receive her healing. There is much more to this story, but this is enough, for now, to illustrate the power of faith.

The eleventh chapter of Hebrews is considered to be a hall of fame for faith. The whole Bible, especially the Gospels, is rich with examples of faith in action. And faith does involve action. Taking a stand against negative reports of contrary evidence is action. Expressing, verbally, what God says in the face of what the world might be trying to say is action. I read the first Psalm that says, "Blessed is the man who walks not in the counsel of the ungodly, nor stands in the path of sinners, nor sits in the seat of the scornful; but his delight is in the law of the Lord, and in His law he meditates day and night. He shall be like a tree planted by the rivers of water that brings forth its fruit in its season, whose leaf also shall not wither; and whatever he does shall prosper" (Ps. 1:1–3). I say, "That is me. Whatever I do shall prosper." That is action and that is faith. (In the next chapter, I will share more details about the power of our words.)

This becomes a very personal thing. We must each find our own promises from the Word. It's the same Word for all of us, but when we find something that relates directly to a circumstance that we face, we can claim it as our own. This fortifies our faith. We have something to pin our hopes to. God said it. He is able to do it. And He is faithful to do what He promises. It is a good idea to write the verses down. Post them in places where they are easy to see often through the day. It is good to be constantly reminded of our promises. The world is constantly trying to say something else. As we stand firm believing God, we demonstrate faith, and that pleases God.

CHAPTER 10

Mind the Mouth

One of the most important areas in life where we must develop some discipline is with what we say. "Death and life are in the power of the tongue, and those who love it will eat its fruit" (Prov. 18:21). I found at least 108 different proverbs that deal with this subject. It would be wise to pay attention to that.

In Genesis, we read about how God created the universe. The materials He used were His words. He simply spoke things into existence. Understand that we are created in the image of God! "Then God said, 'Let us make man in Our image'" (Gen. 1:26). Part of that *image* is the creative power of our words. This may seem a little difficult to grasp at first, but we see it in practice all around us.

In Matthew 8, a Roman centurion asked Jesus to heal his servant. The centurion insisted that Jesus not bother with coming to his home, instead to just *speak a word* and my servant will be healed (Matt. 8:8). An angel appeared to Mary and told her about how she would have a child and name Him Jesus. This began the process of making those things happen. Mary said, "Let it be to me according to your word" (Luke 2:38). She verbally gave her permission. "That if you confess with your mouth the Lord Jesus and believe in your heart that God raised Him from the dead, you will be saved. For with the heart one believes unto righteousness, and with the mouth confession is made unto salvation" (Rom. 10:9–10). Words make things happen.

In the Gospel of Matthew, Jesus spoke to a fig tree, and it withered. The disciples marveled at this, and Jesus told them, "Assuredly, I say to you, if you have faith and do not doubt, you will not only do what was done to the fig tree, but if you say to this mountain, 'Be removed and be cast into the sea,' it will be done" (Matt. 21:21). What was *done* here? Jesus spoke a word, and it happened as He said. He then told His disciples (and us) that it works that way for them (and us) also. Words have power.

God told Moses directly and specifically how to bless. "And the Lord spoke to Moses saying, 'Speak to Aaron and his sons, saying, this is the way you shall bless the children of Israel, say to them: The Lord bless you and keep you; the Lord make His face shine upon you and be gracious to you; the Lord lift up His countenance upon you and give you peace'" (Num. 6:22–26). That's some pretty plain and unambiguous instructions. "This is the way you shall bless…say…"

"Out of the same mouth proceed blessing and cursing" (James 3:10). "You are snared by the words of your mouth" (Prov. 6:2). "The mouth of the foolish is their destruction" (Prov. 10:14). "A harsh word stirs up anger…the mouth of the foolish pours forth foolishness" (Prov. 15:1–2). "A fool's lips enter into contention, and his mouth calls for blows. A fool's mouth is his destruction, and his lips are the snare of his soul. The words of a talebearer are like tasty trifles, and they go down into the inmost body" (Prov. 18:6–8).

I've heard people say things like, "I'm catching a cold." When they say that, it usually comes to pass just as they say. On the other hand, I say things like, "A cold is trying to catch me, but it will not succeed." I often will declare, "Today, I will enjoy the perfect health that Jesus purchased for me at Calvary." And it usually comes to pass just as I say.

When a salesperson approaches a potential client, the first few words spoken will have great impact on how that deal will proceed. When a man courts a woman, with just a few words, he can gain or lose her favor. A good football coach will inspire and motivate his team with words. When a highway patrolman pulls me over, the first few words spoken will make a big difference on how that encounter will go.

Truly, one of the most valuable disciplines a person could ever develop is to stop and think about what we say before words are spoken. Once the words have been spoken, there's no taking them back. If the words spoken were not good, this puts us in a damage control situation. When a confrontation arises, our words can escalate the conflict or diffuse the tensions. "Whoever guards his mouth and tongue keeps his soul from troubles" (Prov. 21:23). "The mouth of the upright will deliver them" (Prov. 12:6). "A soft answer turns away wrath" (Prov. 15:1). "The heart of the wise teaches his mouth and adds learning to his lips. Pleasant words are like a honeycomb, sweetness to the soul and health to the bones" (Prov. 16:23–24).

This isn't some deep theological concept. This is as real and down-to-earth as a thing can be. Our words have power. There's an old expression, "Sticks and stones can break my bones, but words can never hurt me." That may be a convenient way to tell a child not to worry about what someone says to them, but it is not true, and it is a dangerous thought. What we say to and about other people is important, but what we say to and about ourselves is also important.

When we say things like, "I'm no good at math" or "I can't play tennis," we are creating limitations for ourselves. We are giving our permission to failure. It would be better to say, "I have struggled with that in the past, but I believe I can do it." Truly, *life and death are in the power of the tongue.* "The thief does not come except to steal and to kill and to destroy. I have come that they may have life and that they may have it more abundantly" (John 10:10). Do our words bring life and abundance? Or do our words steal, kill, or destroy? This is not a game. This is not some trendy positive mental attitude gimmick. This is real life—as real as it gets. Our words are powerful tools, and we can hurt ourselves and others if we misuse them. We have been given this great toolbox of words. Choose the right tool for the job. A chainsaw will not help if we're changing the oil in our car, and we can't mow the lawn with a box-end wrench. The right tool for the right job works wonders.

It just takes some effort, but it is something that we can all do. It has taken me a long time to make some progress in this area, and I have a long way to go still. The key here is the word *progress*.

JOHN MCLEAN

Whenever a damaging word is not spoken, that is a hurt that didn't happen. Whenever we respond with kindness instead of sarcasm, healing is shared. When a verse of scripture is what comes out instead of some secular cliché, real peace can be imparted. We all have the power to master the tongue.

Chapter 11

Confidence

I recall scenes in movies where someone had to cross a scary bridge. The bridge may be a couple hundred feet long and over a deep canyon with a raging river below. The bridge is made of ropes and old boards. Many of the boards are rotted or missing, and the ropes look rather tattered and worn. But the enemy is approaching, and our hero must get to the other side.

He looks apprehensive and grabs hold of the ropes. He takes a step onto the bridge and gets a sense of how sturdy the bridge is. Will it hold him, or will he fall to his death? This is such a dramatic scene. He must get going. He has to save the princess or something like that. But he must first gain the confidence to cross.

How pleasant it is to get up in the morning and know it will be a good day, to turn the key in the car and know it will start, and I can go to work and know I can do my job well. Confidence is a great thing. I recall times while living in the mountains in California when a storm was approaching. I was confident because I had enough food, water, and cut firewood to survive many days of being snowed in. We certainly must have confidence in the pilot and the plane if we are going to fly somewhere. If we go to the zoo, we must have confidence in the structures that contain the lions, tigers, and bears.

When it comes to confidence in ourselves, it is usually because what we are about to do is something we have been successful at in the past. We have already proven ourselves to be up to the task. If my wife asks me to take out the trash, I know I can do it—I confidently proceed. If I have to change a flat tire, I know I can do it—I've done that many times. Confidence is based on a proven track-record of satisfactory performance. If I base my assurance simply on my belief that I am a wonderful guy who can do anything I put my mind to, then that might be boastful arrogance or, at least, presumption.

One of my favorite proverbs is, "Every word of God is pure. He is a shield to those who put their trust in Him" (Prov. 30:5). I trust God and I trust His Word. This is my confidence. Jeremiah puts it this way, "Blessed is the man who trusts in the Lord, and whose hope is the Lord" (Jer. 17:7). He also says, "Cursed is the man who trusts in man and makes flesh his strength, whose heart departs from the Lord" (Jer. 17:5). Psalms tells us, "It is better to trust in the Lord than to put confidence in man. It is better to trust the Lord than to put confidence in princes" (Ps. 118:8–9).

When crossing a stream on foot, we step from rock to rock. When we do, we make sure that the rock we are about to step on is steady and not wobbly. We are careful to choose where we step because we don't want to fall. In life, we must choose what and who we want to put our trust in. Some people trust what a politician says and trust that the government will take care of them. Some trust in themselves because they have guns, ammo, and survival skills. There are even people who trust in their savings accounts or investment portfolios. It is wise to be prepared, but our trust, our confidence, should be in something better than our preparations. I trust God.

This could be thought of as faith in God. I like to use Abraham and Sarah to explain faith. Abraham was "fully convinced that what He (God) had promised, He was also able to perform" (Rom. 4:21). And Sarah "judged Him faithful Who had promised" (Heb. 11:11). The Word contains many promises from God. These are promises of protection and provision. These are things that we can trust in—things that we can put our confidence in.

God has shown His attitude toward us many times. The first thing He said to Adam and Eve was, "Be blessed and be fruitful" (Gen. 1:28). What He did with Jesus on the cross was the greatest expression of love that could ever be. "For God so loved the world that He gave His only begotten Son that whosoever believes in Him shall not perish but have everlasting life" (John 3:16). We should know that God is on our side. "For I know the thoughts that I think toward you, says the Lord, thoughts of peace and not evil, to give you a future and a hope" (Jer. 29:11). This is what God said to His rebellious Israel while they were in Babylonian captivity.

God loves us. "God is love" (1 John 4:8). "Behold what manner of love the Father has bestowed on us, that we should be called the children of God!" (1 John 3:1) So many times Jesus told us to ask for what we needed or even wanted and ask in His name and God would do it. (Matt 18:18–20; 21:21, 22; John 14:12–14;15:7–8, 16; 16:23–24) To have confidence in God is to simply believe that He is honest. Take a good look at John 3:16, "God so *loved*...that He *gave*..." And we are the object of that love.

There is a passage in First John that I had heard many times before I finally heard all of it. "Now this is the confidence that we have in Him, that if we ask anything according to His will, He hears us" (1 John 5:14). For years, I got stuck on the phrase *according to His will*. Doubt would creep into my thoughts, and I would wonder if maybe my prayers were not exactly according to His will. One day my ears remained open, and I heard the rest of it. "And if we know that He hears us, whatever we ask, we know that we have the petitions that we have asked of Him" (1 John 5:15). The Word, like a soothing ointment, can turn doubt into confidence. All through scripture, He demonstrates His desire. We know His will. It is that we be blessed, fruitful, in perfect health and peace. I know He hears.

"The thief does not come except to steal, and to kill, and to destroy. I have come that they may have life, and that they may have it more abundantly" (John 10:10). God wants us to enjoy an abundant life. Abundance to not only satisfy us, but that we can bless others as well. When the Word says, "By His stripes we are healed" (Isa. 53:5 and 1 Pet. 2:24), we can claim that knowing this is God's will for us. When the word says, "God shall supply all your need according to His riches in glory" (Phil. 4:19), we can claim that knowing this is God's will for us. When the word says, "For by grace you have been saved through faith" (Eph. 2:8), we can claim that knowing this is God's will for us.

To be honest, I don't have a great deal of confidence in myself. I've seen me fail too many times. But I have great confidence in God and in His Word. I have never seen Him fail. And I have seen Him show Himself strong and true on many occasions in my own life and others. The amazing, the difficult, the miraculous, the impossible (for man)—I've seen God do all these things. Supernatural healing and provision, just the right words to say at a difficult moment, guidance and warnings at times of imminent danger—I've experienced all these things myself.

I don't put my confidence in God just because I've seen or experienced things. I put my trust in God because of His promises, because of the truth of His Word. I love the lyrics of an old gospel song, "Blessed assurance, Jesus is mine. Oh what a foretaste of glory divine." I wrote one a few years ago that said, "I have this confidence in the truth or Your word. I made my prayers, and I know that You heard. And I know You love me and that You want to bless. I'd be a fool to expect something less."

Be confident. Trust God. Know that your confidence and trust are on a firm foundation. And become ever more familiar with that foundation by reading His Word daily.

Chapter 12

Prayer

Perhaps the most important element of a Christian life is prayer. Family therapists say that communication is a key to a happy marriage. Likewise, communication is a key to our relationship with God. We have His Word. We have anointed ministers who teach and preach that Word. We also have direct access to God Himself so we can, and should, have two-way conversations with Him whenever we need to.

Prayers in public can seem so formal. Ministers will often use such fancy or Bible-sounding words. But prayer is simply a conversation with God. It is as if we climbed onto the lap of our loving Father, and as He hugs us, we tell Him what's on our mind. He loves us and wants to have this encounter. He wants to hear our heart and then give us what is needed.

The words used are not particularly important. We do not have to open up with, "We beseech thee to hear us, oh Lord." A simple and yet effective prayer might simply be, "Lord, save me!" The only difference between how we would speak with God and how we would speak with a close friend is that God already knows what's going on. We don't have to fill Him in on the details.

In the Gospels, we read how Jesus would often get away from the crowds, or even His disciples, and pray. This was His alone time with His Father. For a lot of people, prayer is just something said before a meal or something that ministers do at a church service. But to have a satisfying and productive relationship, we must communicate often. Prayers can be at bedtime, in the morning, routine prayer times, spontaneous moments—whatever suits our needs.

There's no special formula or certain words that *make it work*. There's no magic incantation like, *abracadabra* or *open sesame*. It is just a conversation with our Father God. When I speak to my wife, I usually say something like this, "Hey, sweetie, I'd like to do this today..." It doesn't have to be anything more formal than that. He is God, the Creator of the universe and the Possessor of all things, but He is also our Father. "Behold what manner of love the Father has bestowed on us, that we should be called the children of God" (1 John 3:1).

The original disciples watched Jesus pray, and then they asked Him, "Lord, teach us to pray" (Luke 11:1). "So He said to them, 'When you pray, say: Our Father in heaven, hallowed be Your name. Your kingdom come, Your will be done on earth as it is in heaven. Give us day by day our daily bread, and forgive us our sins, for we also forgive everyone who is indebted to us. And do not lead us into temptation but deliver us from the evil one" (Luke 11:2–4). This prayer is also documented in Matthew 6. The wording is a little different there, and different Bible translations will word things a little differently also. But Jesus was not giving us a formal series of specific words like a pledge of allegiance. He was giving us a simple example for prayer. This is often referred to as The Lord's Prayer.

Jesus said to *pray like this*, but this was not intended to be something recited as a religious ritual. The elements of this prayer are good ingredients for a conversation with a loving Father. Acknowledging God for Who He is, praying that His will be done, and asking for provision and deliverance are all good things. It's all right to recite this. However, effective prayer is a conversation not a recital. It serves little purpose when, at work, if I need to discuss some matter and all I do is recite our company's mission statement. When I need to discuss something with my wife, I don't just recite our wedding vows. Don't make this a *religious* practice—it's much more important and personal than that. Let go of a notion of *formality* and think in terms of *intimacy*.

"And when you pray, you shall not be like the hypocrites. For they love to pray standing in the synagogues and on the corners of the street that they may be seen by men. Assuredly, I say to you, they have their reward" (Matt. 6:5). Prayers can be made in public, but it is still a conversation with God and not just an opportunity to show off some measure of spirituality.

It is most effective to pray according to scripture. By that I mean that is always better if we have a good foundation from the Bible to make our requests. "And whatever things you ask in prayer, believing you will receive" (Matt. 21:22). We must be confident that what we are praying for is something good and right, or we might not really believe it. "If any of you lacks wisdom, let him ask of God, who gives to all liberally and without reproach, and it will be given to him. But let him ask in faith, with no doubting, for he who doubts is like a wave of the sea driven and tossed by the wind. For let not that man suppose that he will receive anything from the Lord: he is a double-minded man, unstable in all his ways" (James 1:5–8).

We must check our motives. "You ask and do not receive, because you ask amiss, that you may spend it on your pleasures" (James 4:3). This is not to say that it is wrong to pray for anything pleasant. God wants us to enjoy life. But I don't waste my time praying that God would give me a new Corvette so that I could meet lots of pretty young girls.

It's good to know a couple other things about prayer. First, there are many things that people pray for that God has already done. As believers, we are forgiven of all sins—the blood of Jesus has washed all that away. When we ask Him to forgive us for something we recently did, we are expressing doubt about what was already done. "Through the offering of the body of Jesus Christ once for all" (Heb. 10:10). When we know that we have sinned or done something inappropriate, we should repent (which simply means to turn from that). A better prayer would be to simply thank Him for the gift of grace and for Him to help us do better next time.

"Is anyone among you suffering? Let him pray. Is anyone cheerful? Let him sing psalms. Is anyone among you sick? Let him call for the elders of the church and let them pray over him, anointing him with oil in the name of the Lord, and the prayer of faith will save the sick, and the Lord will raise him up. And if he has committed sins, he will be forgiven" (James 5:13–15). James goes on to give this example, "Elijah was a man with a nature like ours; and he prayed earnestly that it would not rain; and it did not rain on the land for three years and six months. And he prayed again, and the heavens gave rain, and the earth produced its fruit" (James 5:17–18).

I remember a time when I had a bad cold and was suffering all the classic symptoms of a runny nose and so on. I was in my car at lunch time. (This was my practice when I worked.) I remembered this verse of scripture and thought, "Hey, I'm the elder in this car right now. I'll do this." So I put some oil on my forehead and prayed for the healing. The next day, I realized that every symptom was gone—I was, in fact, healed! Another time, I prayed to be healed of arthritis. This was something that many of my relatives suffered from, and it appeared to be trying to strike me also. It hurt to play the guitar and that is how I worshipped. All I knew at the time was that I didn't want to be hindered from worshiping God and that Jesus is my healer. Praise God! I am healed. That was over twenty years ago, and I'm still playing guitar.

I've heard it said that we should not speak to God about our mountain but speak to the mountain about God. "If you say to this mountain, 'Be removed and cast into the sea,' it will be done" (Matt. 21:21). Jesus didn't *pray* for healing—he *commanded* healing. We have that authority now also. I have commanded healing also. Either way, God is rich in His mercy and has paid dearly for our healing. Be led by the Spirit.

A farmer might pray that God would bless his fields this season, but he still has to work the land. I might pray that a neighbor or coworker would come to know Jesus, but I still reach out to them to show them kindness, generosity, and be a good witness of a loving Savior. There are things that God has told us to do. When we feel incapable of doing things that we know He wants us to do, we simply pray for the guidance, strength, or whatever is needed. We should never feel embarrassed or ashamed by what we think we cannot do. God is glorified when ordinary people do extraordinary things.

Finally, we pray in the name of Jesus. What does that mean? Jesus told us to pray or ask the Father in His name (John 14:14; John 15:16). Jesus has given us something like power of attorney. When we pray in His name, God hears as if it was Jesus speaking with His Father.

Paul says to, "Pray without ceasing" (1 Thess. 5:17). This does not mean that we spend our days on our knees praying over and over. It means that we can and should be constantly aware of our connection with God. The moment something comes up, we can pray about it. When I am driving, and a traffic light stays green long enough for me to pass through an intersection without having to stop, I say, "Thank You, Lord." The moment I see or hear about someone in need, I can instantly be in prayer about it.

There are many more things to learn about prayer. The bottom line is to pray. Pray to the Father, in the name of Jesus. Pray believing. And pray whenever and wherever it's either needed or desired. God is never too busy to hear from His children.

Chapter 13

Giving

In that verse that we are all so familiar with now, John 3:16, is found a fundamental principle of the Christian life—giving. "For God so loved…that He gave…" God loved, so He gave. It's His nature. He is love and He gives. That is becoming our nature also as we learn to follow Him.

In the fourth chapter of Genesis, we read about Cain and Able, the second generation of mankind. The first two things mentioned about them was what they did (did for a living, so to speak) and what they offered as a sacrifice to God. Cain was a tiller of the ground. Able tended the sheep. Cain offered fruit to God, and Able offered of the first born of his flock.

I'm not going into the story of Cain and Able and how their offerings were received, but I do want to point out the concept of *making an offering*. It has nothing to do with church as we know it. It has nothing to do with the law (there was no Mosaic law yet in the days of Cain and Able). It was simply a natural thing to do. They were given everything and they, in turn, wanted to give something back as a gesture of worship and honor.

Another very early (prelaw) mention of giving, or tithing, is mentioned in Genesis 14. A leader named Chedorlaomer had conquered the towns of Sodom and Gomorrah (yes, the famous Sodom and Gomorrah, before they were destroyed) and taken Lot, Abraham's nephew, captive. Abraham then took his men to fight Chedorlaomer and defeat him. They rescued Lot and recovered all that had been stolen from Sodom and Gomorrah.

Right after this they meet Melchizedek, who was described as the King of Salem and the priest of God Most High (see Gen. 14:18). Melchizedek gave them bread and wine and blessed them. "And he gave him a tithe of all" (Gen. 14:20). What is implied here is that Abraham gave to Melchizedek a tenth of the goods that were recovered in the battle. A tithe is simply a tenth, a tenth of the *spoils of battle*. Those spoils were simply the property of the kings of Sodom and Gomorrah that Abraham had recovered. But, nonetheless, the concept of giving a portion is displayed here.

Later God gave to Moses the Law—the Mosaic Law also known as the Old Covenant. All the details were expressly laid out about the Levites, who were one of the twelve tribes—the twelve sons of Jacob. The Levites owned no land as individuals; they were devoted to the work of the ministry. It was part of the law that people involved with certain occupations were to bring a tenth of their earnings and give it to the Levites for their provision. There were many other offerings and sacrifices that were to be made to God also. Here again we see the biblical concept of giving played out now in a practical way.

If we skip forward to the time when Paul was ministering to the early church, we still see this concept of giving in action. There were people who were suffering in Jerusalem, whom Paul wanted to support. As he went from church to church, he would take an offering from those people to take back to Jerusalem. Churches at that time were humble gatherings of believers who met in peoples' homes to worship and break bread together. What was important at that time was that they would come together, like family, to encourage one another and support one another with prayer or whatever else may be needed.

The modern churches that we see today have sprung from this tradition. Churches have grown from these humble gatherings of believers—sometimes in secret because of intense persecution—to huge ornate cathedrals. The modern concept is a nice facility where people gather every Sunday for worship and a word from a preacher. Regardless of how big the facility is, it costs money to maintain it.

Just like how the Levites had to be supported by the tithes, modern churches are supported by the giving of the congregants. Anyone who is a member of a church and receiving whatever benefits are associated with that fellowship is responsible for helping to support it.

As Christians, that is to say as partakers of the New Covenant of grace, we are no longer bound by the Mosaic Law and the specific ordinances described therein. But the concepts of giving, making a sacrifice, and supporting the church and people in need have not changed any more than the concepts of not murdering or stealing. It is good to give. To give is a natural outpouring of love. "It is more blessed to give than to receive" (Acts 20:35). But there are a few things to be aware of in this regard.

The most important thing to be aware of is that we do not (and cannot) gain some measure of favor with God by giving. We can never *achieve* anything with God or *merit* grace. There is no such thing as *positioning yourself* to receive from God by giving. God loves, so He gives. Grace is a gift and not a wage. God does not work on a quid-pro-quo basis—His favor cannot be bought. It is very important to understand this. We must have faith in God and never have faith in what we *do* or give.

We are responsible for our homes and families. Never give to a ministry if it means putting the family in jeopardy. It is good to develop the financial discipline so that a tenth of our earnings can be given away. That is to say that if we learn to function well on ninety percent of our earnings, it frees up a good amount for the work of the ministry. This keeps the horse before the cart, and it is amazing how resources become available for more and more giving while at the same time properly supporting the family. If this is all new, and it is not realistic to give ten percent of the family earnings right now, don't do it. It's all right. Work toward that, in a way, that is workable with the family budget. Trust God. He is the provider. We work hard. We give what we can. But our faith for our family's provision should always be in God, and not in our jobs, our hard work, or our giving.

We are constantly confronted with impassioned pleas for financial support. Evangelists on TV will boast about how their message of hope is broadcast around the world, and they need our support. The church we attend needs a new roof or an expansion to the nursery or whatever and, of course, that requires money. Everywhere we look there are needs—often serious needs. Be wise and listen to God for His direction. There have been many times when God has told me to give a specific amount of money to someone or even give a car. So when that happens, I do my best to obey. Listen to the voice of God, not men.

Whenever we hear anyone quote the Old Testament or speak in terms of a requirement, be leery. Anytime we are told that we must exercise our faith in God's provision by giving, be cautious. God cannot be manipulated—although we can be. Giving is good. Supporting the local church is good. Supporting other ministries that help people is good. I have heard it said, and I have found this to be true that, "You can't out give God." There is a principal that transcends all social, ethnic, and religious lines, and that is referred to as the principle of sowing and reaping. An example is, "A man who has friends must himself be friendly" (Prov. 18:24).

Like with Cain and Able, we give because all has been given to us. Like Abraham, we give as a form of worship and honor. And like the people Paul ministered to, we give because other people are hurting, and we can help. This is different from when the government takes taxes out of our paychecks or when someone steals money or property from us. To give is a willful voluntary action and not the satisfaction of an obligation. To give is good. To give is a natural outpouring of love. Be wise but be a cheerful giver.

CHAPTER 14

Worship

As a musician, this is one of my favorite subjects. All throughout the Bible, we see worship. So much of the Mosaic Law was centered on how various ceremonies were to be conducted. The largest book in the Bible is Psalms—the hymnal of the Scriptures. As believers, we naturally want to give honor to God. Music is one way to do this.

I like to think of Christian music as being praise, worship, or bait. My own simple definitions are these—praise is singing about God. Worship is singing to God. And bait is singing in such a way that it might draw unbelievers into a relationship with God. The subject of this music is how good God is and how wonderful it is to know Jesus. We sing about His grace and mercy. We sing about His might and His faithfulness. And we express our love and appreciation in song.

Praise music is typically up tempo and enthusiastic, while worship music is often quieter and more reflective. Although neither of those statements are always true. I like to think of it this way—if I stand in front of a group of people and say, "My wife is wonderful." That would be like praise. But if I whisper in her ear, "I love you." That would be like worship.

There is something wonderful about getting together with other people and praising God. Jesus said, "For where two or three are gathered together in My name, I am there in the midst of them"

(Matt. 18:20). It is not as if we are conjuring up a spirit. As we gather, He is there. But there is often an electrifying experience when we praise Him as a church. And evidently, He enjoys it. Praise is a powerful force in the spirit realm. Demonic entities cannot handle it. As we praise, those things that have been trying to hold us down have to flee. This kind of environment can present a great opportunity for healing and deliverance.

Singing can become an extremely personal thing as well. When we have taken our attention off all the cares of life and focus on Jesus, it becomes an intensely intimate moment. I remember when I first began to experience this. Tears would stream down my face, and it seemed like Jesus was holding me in His arms. I didn't know what was going on, and I was a little embarrassed by crying in public. I have since learned not to worry about that. Worship, like this, is a beautiful moment—to be embraced by the Creator of the universe. He is a loving and affectionate God.

I have heard it said that we were created to worship God. "Thou art worthy, O Lord, to receive glory and honor and power; for thou hast created all things, and for thy pleasure they are and were created" (Rev. 4:11 KJV). It becomes another of those great Christian paradoxes. The more we bless Him, the more we are blessed. Worship is what it's all about. To me, it is like working hard to provide a nice home for the family, and then going home for the evening to just enjoy being with the wife and kids. We work and do all the other things, but there comes a time for us to indulge in the fruits of those labors and experience the love of the family.

Worship is not just music and songs. Over the years, there have been some things that I have taken upon myself to do around the church. I noticed weeds popping up in the cracks of the pavement of our church parking lot. I thought it looked a little sloppy, so on a day off, I brought a string trimmer and some weed spray and took care of the matter. I was hoping that nobody would see me. I just wanted our church to look nice. But one of our pastors came out to thank me. I just said that this is a way that I worshipped God. Our church (and I think most churches) is full of people who do things like this.

A life of giving, sharing, and loving is a life of worship. To lead a congregation in a Sunday morning song service can be worship. To help a stranger change a flat tire can be worship also. Anytime we do anything for no reason other than to express our love for God, we are worshipping. To honor God by loving the things that He loves is worship. To be a blessing to people because God loves them, and we love Him, is worship. It becomes something that we don't think about. It becomes a natural thing to simply let His love for other people flow through us. This is worship. This is giving honor and glory to God.

Back to the music, which is my favorite part of worship, I am not a particularly good singer. I also am intermediate at best in terms of proficiency on the guitar. But shortly after getting saved, I was taken under the wing, so to speak, by a worship leader. Joe was a great mentor for me. He had me join the praise team at our little church, and he showed by example what it meant to worship—in all the ways described above. I have been a part of church praise and worship teams ever since—almost thirty years now.

I have played guitar with very large orchestras full of professional-quality musicians and a big choir. I have led worship services by myself. At times I was the guy who knew what we were doing and leading the group. At times I was just tagging along and hoping that I didn't mess anything up or cause a distraction. The settings have been large cathedral-like sanctuaries, small fellowship halls, prisons, people's homes, and around a campfire. None of these things have mattered.

It is not the musicians. It is not the setting. It isn't even the songs. It is a spirit of worship that makes it special. Anyone can buy a ticket and hear great performers make music. But genuine worship is something that cannot be bought. This is an experience that transcends the songs. We connect with God on a heart-to-heart level—or more accurately a spirit-to-spirit level.

I am honored to be known as a Christian. That is a reputation that I find flattering. But there could be no greater honor for me than to be known as a worshipper. That is a crown I'd love lay at the feet of Jesus someday.

Chapter 15

Fasting

Another activity among Christians is fasting. To fast has nothing to do with velocity. It is simply going without something. A great example of this is, "And when He had fasted forty days and forty nights, afterward He was hungry" (Matt. 4:2). Jesus went forty days and nights without eating.

As you can imagine, He became very hungry. I would think He was extremely hungry, and this is when the devil tempted Him (unsuccessfully). When I first became a Christian, I wondered what the purpose or benefit was for fasting.

As a kid, I remember that meat was not served in the school cafeteria on Fridays. There was also the religious tradition of Lent. All I knew about that was that before Easter some people would abstain from something that they usually enjoyed. I would hear things like, "I gave up coffee for Lent." These were examples of fasting.

These are religious practices and as such are things to be aware of, but they are, by no means, a requirement. Remember the requirements are simply to believe in Jesus, and the finished work of the cross. Beyond that, we are to love and not judge people. But there are benefits to fasting—both physical and spiritual.

I have read many reports about the health benefits of fasting. Not necessarily forty days and nights without any food whatsoever, but for a day or maybe two. This gives the body a chance to cleanse itself. Also to go without a particular thing that is consumed routinely is good to make sure that it isn't becoming an unhealthy habit. "All things are lawful for me, but all things are not helpful. All things are lawful for me, but I will not be brought under the power of any" (1 Cor. 6:16).

We have been redeemed from all the dietary restrictions of the Old Covenant. It is now lawful, as Paul puts it, to eat pork. It may be lawful to have a glass of wine with a meal or eat chocolate or even smoke, but fasting these things can help us keep that practice in perspective. We would never want to be controlled by an urge to eat a dessert after every meal or any other practice that becomes an unhealthy habit.

There is also a spiritual benefit to fasting. Right off the bat, I want to declare that, as New Covenant believers, we cannot move or manipulate God by our fasting. It is an absolutely silly thing to think that we could ever say, "Oh, God, look at what I have given up for you." I mean, really, look at what He has given for us. Aside from the benefit of making sure that we are not *brought under the power* of some habit, there is something else. It is a matter of trust. It is the nature of our flesh to want food. Our bodies will demand it. When we go a day without eating, we are telling our bodies that they are not in charge.

"Moreover, when you fast, do not be like the hypocrites, with a sad countenance. For they disfigure their faces that they may appear to men to be fasting. Assuredly, I say to you, they have their reward. But you, when you fast, anoint your head and wash your face, so that you do not appear to men to be fasting, but to your Father which is in the secret place; and your Father which sees in secret will reward you openly" (Matt. 6:16–18). According to Jesus, there is a benefit to be received openly from God if we are discreet about this practice of fasting.

I used to fast on Wednesdays. One time, a fellow that I worked with came back from his lunch break with an extra hamburger from the restaurant next door. He offered it to me, so I thanked him, but declined. He went on to insist that I take it. It made no sense to him that I wouldn't, but I didn't want to say that I was fasting. My coworker had previously shared that he was a recovering addict who was going through a twelve-step process called Narcotics Anonymous. This gave me a way to explain discreetly and effectively.

I related it to the addiction that he was fighting. I told him about how my flesh has its appetites also and how my flesh has gotten me into trouble with its cravings. He was right there with me, nodding his head—he understood that. I went on to explain that it was a matter of discipline that I go a day without eating just to make sure that my own body knew that I was the boss and not it. He was well aware of the distinction between our bodies, or our flesh, and our spirit, or our inner man—the real us. This explanation made perfect sense to him, and the matter was settled.

This explanation helped me understand also. It's as if I was teaching myself a great principle of fasting. It isn't a great sacrifice made in an effort to gain God's favor. We already have that. It was a matter of discipline. I had to show my own body who's the boss. I also had to remind myself about Who is the sustainer of my life. By not eating for a day, I was declaring that God is the one who gives me life and not me.

One time, I went two days without eating, and to be honest, I was a little disappointed with how easy it was. So I went a third day without eating. Still, I wasn't experiencing great pains, but I was becoming rather weak. I no longer go without eating on Wednesday. I don't like to let things like that become some sort of religious practice that loses its meaning. However, whenever I think some routine practice or indulgence is trying to take over, I'll stop it for a time. Discipline must be maintained; otherwise, freedom is lost.

"The disciples of John and the Pharisees were fasting. Then they came and said to Him, 'Why do the disciples of John and of the Pharisees fast, but Your disciples do not fast?' And Jesus said to them, 'Can the friends of the bridegroom fast while the bridegroom is with them? As long as they have the bridegroom with them, they cannot fast. But the days will come when the bridegroom will be taken away from them, and then they will fast on those days. No one sews a piece of un-shrunk cloth on an old garment; or else the new piece pulls away from the old and the tear is made worse. And no one puts new wine into old wineskins; or else the new wine bursts the wineskins, the wine is spilled, and the wineskins are ruined. But new wine must be put into new wineskins'" (Mark 2:18–22).

Moses and Elijah both fasted for forty days, like Jesus did. But they were under the Old Covenant. Jesus wanted to put this religious practice in its place. At the time, fasting was a thing that religious people did to show off. Jesus was declaring that fasting might be something that was to be done, but only on occasion—and privately as a simple expression of humility. Often churches will unite for a time of prayer and fasting. People will commit to abstaining from something like TV, social media, soda pop, or whatever for a period of time. This practice is to bring unity among a body of believers for focused prayer—usually about major decisions that the church was facing or for our world or community.

The bottom line here is that fasting is a good practice if done correctly. It is for health benefits, personal discipline, church unity, and bringing oneself closer to our loving Father. It should never be a meaningless religious practice for the purpose of satisfying a requirement. And fasting should never be done in an effort to move or impress God.

Chapter 16

Serving

Another important part of this journey is serving. Now we are believers in Jesus. Saved, as Paul would say; born again, as Jesus would say; redeemed as the Old Testament would say; or Christians, as the world would say. But what do we *do* now?

Many things have changed. Our values, attitudes, and habits may change over time. Our ultimate destination has certainly changed. But many things remain the same. We still have the same basic needs and interests. We still work, pay rent, raise children, maintain the yard, or whatever we had to do before. One of the main desires that all people have for their life is to accomplish something of value. This also has not changed. Nobody would want it etched on their gravestone, "Here lies one who ate and slept. The eating's lost but the sleep he kept."

The first command that God gave to any man was, "Be fruitful and multiply" (Gen. 1:28). This applies to all mankind, and it does not just mean have lots of children. By becoming a Christian, we have not been drafted into *the service* and required to perform tasks. We were performing tasks anyway—now those tasks may have greater value. We haven't been given work to do so much as we now have been given a greater purpose.

All of us have a unique combination of natural abilities, skills, aptitudes, and interests. It was so for Jeremiah. "Before I formed you in the womb, I knew you; before you were born, I sanctified you; I ordained you a prophet to the nations" (Jer. 1:5). The Psalmist understood this as well. "For I am fearfully and wonderfully made..." (Ps. 139:14). Each one of us is God's handiwork. He intricately formed each of us in special ways for special purposes.

Many years ago something caught my eye about the Israelites coming out of Egypt. "See, I have called by name Bezalel the son of Uri, the son of Hur, of the tribe of Judah. And I have filled him with the Spirit of God, in wisdom, in understanding, in knowledge, and in all manner of workmanship, to design artistic works, to work in gold, in silver, in bronze, in cutting jewels for setting, in carving wood, and to work in all manner of workmanship. And I, indeed I, have appointed with them Aholiab the son of Ahisamach, of the tribe of Dan; and I have put wisdom in the hearts of all the gifted artisans, that they may make all that I have commanded you" (Exo. 31:2–6).

"And Bezalel and Aholiab, and every gifted artisan in whom the Lord has put wisdom and understanding, to know how to do all manner of work for the service of the sanctuary, shall do according to all that the Lord has commanded. Then Moses called Bezalel and Aholiab, and every gifted artisan in whose heart the Lord had put wisdom, everyone whose heart was stirred, to come and do the work" (Exo. 36:1–2), Not only did God give them skills, He stirred their hearts to want to do the work.

These people were sheep herders and farmers. They didn't know how to make a tabernacle like God wanted, so God gave them the knowledge and skills necessary. In like manner, God has a church to build now. And we may not have all the skills or knowledge to do the work, but don't worry about that. If God has stirred our hearts, He will give us whatever is needed for the completion of what He has called us to do. We must just show up to work. "On this rock, I will build My church, and the gates of hell will not prevail against it. And I will give you the keys of the kingdom of heaven" (Matt. 16:18–19).

"For we are His workmanship created in Christ Jesus for good works, which God prepared beforehand that we should walk in them" (Eph. 2:10). Before I was saved, I liked to party. I played guitar—mostly blues and rock and roll. Believe it or not, those are transferable skills. When we become a Christian, we are still us, and we still come in contact with the same people we used to. Now we carry with us something wonderful that we can share with them. I saw a sign in a church parking lot that faced people as they left the church that said, "You are now entering your mission field." Be somewhat careful about this, however. I no longer hang out in bars or go to the same kind of parties that I used to, nor do I encourage anyone else to. I don't think it's a good idea to fish in water where I can drown.

I heard a speaker make a very brief presentation once. He went to the podium and said, "What are you doing...for God's sake?" Then he went and sat down. That's about as succinct as can be. In 1 Corinthians 12, Paul describes a variety of *gifts* or offices. "And God has appointed these in the church; first apostles, second prophets, third teachers, after that miracles, then gifts of healings, helps, administrations, varieties of tongues" (1 Cor. 12:28). In this chapter, Paul makes a lengthy comparison of the functions of people in the church and the functions of parts of the human body. He stressed the point that all the parts are vital to good health even if they are not noticeable or attractive.

"Now concerning spiritual gifts, brethren, I do not want you to be ignorant. There are diversities of gifts, but the same Spirit. There are differences of ministries, but the same Lord. And there are diversities of activities, but the same God who works all in all: for to one is given the word of wisdom through the Spirit, to another the word of knowledge through the same Spirit, to another faith by the same Spirit, to another gifts of healings by the same Spirit, to another the working of miracles, to another prophecy, to another discerning of spirits, to another the interpretation of tongues. But one and the same Spirit works all these things, distributing to each one individually as He wills" (1 Cor. 12:1, 4–11).

To some degree, all believers have all these gifts, but we each have one or two of these in a much greater way. There are tests or surveys that are available to help determine what our own individual Spiritual gifts are. See your pastor or look online for this. "Having then gifts differing according to the grace that is given to us, let us use them: if prophecy, let us prophecy in proportion to our faith; or ministry, let us use it in our ministering; he who teaches, in teaching;

he who exhorts, in exhortation; he who gives, with liberality; he who leads, with diligence; he who shows mercy, with cheerfulness" (Rom. 12:6–8).

These gifts are nothing to boast about. They are not merit badges that we have earned. Note how Paul describes them as *grace that is given*. Neither are these unpleasant tasks that have been assigned to us. These are things that were hardwired into our personalities before we were born. These are things that may have been in operation in our lives for years. Now we know why. Now they have greater purpose.

As members of a local church, we have some measure of responsibility to chip in and help with the work that needs to be done to maintain and operate that church. There are many areas for service in most any church. There is help needed in the nursery. There are greeters, ushers, sound and lighting technicians, musicians, security people, ground maintenance workers. A pastor should not be expected to do all these things by himself. Don't think of church as a service that we subscribe to, but a service where we participate. Have some skin in the game. Embrace and take ownership of the mission of the church.

I have found that there is no greater satisfaction in life than to find a suitable place of service and then to just serve with all my heart. Many times I have been tired, my back hurt, my hands hurt, and my throat hurt, but when I stood in front of a group to minister, I was able to play, sing, and speak just fine. I may have been tired afterward, but I was energized to serve. I was *anointed* to do the work I was called to do. I have never considered myself to be particularly good at anything either. But that does not matter. I've heard it said that "God doesn't call the equipped, He equips the called."

Service is not *paying back*. There is no way to repay God for the gifts given to us. What could we give God anyway? He already has it all. He has angels to do for Him whatever He wants done. Service is satisfying a God-given purpose for our lives. It is also satisfying a natural desire to accomplish something of value. When I was a child, there was a large department store in town called May Co. On the top of their building were four very large M's in lights. My grandfather was the electrician who wired those Ms. I always thought that was a big accomplishment. It may have been just another job to him, but those lights shone brightly long after his passing.

We may or may not ever be elected to some sort of a hall of fame. We may never even be acknowledged for anything at all. We might not even feel appreciated by our friends or family. But none of that really matters. Life is short, but we live forever. I sincerely hope that one day each of us will hear, "Well done, My good and faithful servant; you have been faithful over a few things, I will make you ruler over many things. Enter into the joy of your Lord" (Matt. 25:23). I've heard it asked, "If you knew you only had twenty-four hours to live, what would you do?" When Jesus knew He only had twenty-four hours to live, He washed His disciple's feet.

Chapter 17

Empathy

We now are vessels or containers of the Holy Spirit. Moses had built an ark that contained the stone tablets that the Ten Commandments were written on as well as some other artifacts. The big thing was that the power or presence of God was in that box as well. This was symbolic of us and how that same power or presence of God is carried about within us.

"Abide in Me, and I in You" (John 15:4). "But we have this treasure in earthen vessels, that the excellence of the power may be of God and not of us" (2 Cor. 4:7). "Do you not know that you are the temple of God and that the Spirit of God dwells in you?" (1 Cor. 3:16). We are not alone. It is not just some metaphor that we asked Jesus to come and live in our heart. His Spirit now resides within us.

We know also that there are some characteristics of God's personality that are known as the *fruit of the Spirit*. "But the fruit of the Spirit is love, joy, peace, long-suffering, kindness, goodness, faithfulness, gentleness, self-control. Against such there is no law" (Gal. 5:22–23). These are not the fruit of us, but the fruit of the Holy Spirit. As our nature takes a back seat to God's nature, these qualities begin to show in us.

In times of loss, we might experience joy. In times of trouble, we might experience peace. We might even be kind or gentle with people we don't like. This is God's personality, the fruit of His Spirit shining brighter than that or our own. But there is a very big thing that will shine in us (if we let it), and that is empathy. I would define that as simply caring about other people. Empathy would be when I see someone suffer, it almost feels like I am suffering with them. I may not know them at all, but I care deeply that they are hurting.

The first fruit mentioned above is love. Remember God is not *a god* who loves. God is love. (1 John 4:8 and 4:16) In the lyrics of popular music or literature, love is a feeling or emotion. In reality, love is a person. Love is God. God *is* love. Whatever perceptions we may have had from personal or cultural exposure or conditioning should be clarified by knowing God, who is love. When we love someone, we tend to care about the things that they care about. God loves people—all people. So we who love God tend to love all people also. We will even love people who we, otherwise, might not like.

Our attitudes to other people change. When we see people who appear to be indulging in a sinful or deviant lifestyle, we are not disgusted or offended by them, thinking that we are somehow morally superior. (Perhaps we might be disgusted by the sin, but not by them) Instead, it breaks our heart that they are lost and hurting. "Brethren, if a man is overtaken in any trespass, you who are spiritual restore such a one in a spirit of gentleness, considering yourself lest you also be tempted" (Gal. 6:1). None of us was or is all that spotless in ourselves. "For with the heart one *believes* unto righteousness" (Rom. 10:10).

James says, "For whoever shall keep the whole law, and yet stumble in one point, he is guilty of all" (James 2:10). I like to think of it this way, whatever sin I think someone else has committed is small compared to the sin of me thinking mine is any less. If anyone is saved, they are saved by grace through faith in Jesus—that's it. Empathy, or God's love pouring through us, overrides a natural urge to judge and replaces it with a hunger to help. When a bucket full of water is shaken or disturbed, what comes out? If we are full of love and are shaken or disturbed, what comes out?

Another manifestation of empathy is intercessory prayer. "Bear one another's burdens, and so fulfill the law of Christ" (Gal. 6:2). This verse came alive to me one day, many years ago. I had been saved for less than a year, and I was attending a small church. One of the young boys in our church was seriously injured and was in the hospital, so some of the older people gathered at the church to pray. Earlier that day, this young boy ran across a busy street and was hit by a car. I had the time and came to join them in prayer. I had never done anything like this before, and I did not know what to expect. Some people were kneeling; some were standing or walking around the room. I sat at a table and began to pray.

As I was praying for healing, my thoughts drifted toward the boy's little sister who had witnessed the incident. So I began to pray for her peace also. All of a sudden, I was overwhelmed by feelings of terror. It was as if I was seeing my own brother flying up in the air and then landing on the pavement. She was horrified at the sight and very concerned about her brother. These were not my feelings, but I was feeling them nonetheless. I was helping her carry a very heavy burden. I was fulfilling the law of Christ.

Since then, I have noticed many times when someone would come forward for prayer after a church service, I would experience something similar. While the pastor or whoever was praying with someone, I would sit in my chair and pray also. Of course, the matter that was being prayed about was not known to me since it was a private matter shared only with whoever they were praying with. (Praying *in the Spirit*, as Paul puts it, is handy for times like this.) Feelings of pain, anguish, shame, or distress would come over me. Feelings that were alien to me but real feelings—their feelings anyway. They were the burdens that those people were carrying, and I was helping them with the weight of it.

The shortest verse in the Bible is "Jesus wept" (John 11:35). The context of this verse tells us a lot about empathy. Lazarus had died four days prior and had been placed in a tomb. When Jesus showed up, Mary, Lazarus's sister, and many others were weeping and mourning. I've heard people say that Jesus wept because of their lack of faith, but I believe He was simply empathizing with them. He was helping them carry the burden of sorrow.

When a friend shares the hurt of a loss, we sit with them and offer comfort. Often that comfort is just to be with them as they suffer. We don't judge them. We don't try to *fix* it. We just sit with them while they deal with it and to listen while they share their hurt and actually care about them is a big help. A hug can work miracles. It is nothing short of the mark of a psychopath to hear about someone's hurt and just think, "Oh well, it doesn't matter to me." We care. We love. Even if we don't think we do, God does, and He is operating through us. This is empathy.

Empathy is not something that we *do* so much as it is something that we *allow* to be done through us by God. One morning, I woke up hearing, "You are blessed. The hand of God is upon you. People around you are blessed because healing, joy, and peace flow through you—not from you, but through you, because you are blessed. The hand of God is upon you." At first, I thought, "Cool. I'm blessed." Then it settled in just what a responsibility this is. People around me need what God wants to pour through me.

All believers are blessed like this, and God has much love and grace that He wants to pour through all of us. Other people desperately need it. We are not special in ourselves, but what we contain is very special. Each of us have unique opportunities to be in different situations or environments where people need what God wants to give to people. This is empathy—a good thing.

CHAPTER 18

Religion and Works

Something to be careful of is the notion that we must do things to receive the grace of God. The grace of God is a gift and not a reward for service. We do things as a result of or in response to that gift. But we do not do things in order to receive that gift or position ourselves to be worthy to receive that gift.

Throughout history, people have followed pagan religions. Usually, sacrifices were made to pagan deities in hopes of gaining their favor for good weather, abundant crops, or fertility. Some cultures worshipped the sun or other celestial bodies. Some would fabricate a statue to worship. "The idols of the nations are silver and gold, the work of men's hands. They have mouths, but they do not speak; eyes they have, but they do not see; they have ears, but they do not hear; nor is there any breath in their mouths. Those who make them are like them; so is everyone who trusts in them" (Ps. 135:15–18).

We might not bow to or worship a fabricated idol or sacrifice our children in a fire. But we sometimes fall into a similar type of bondage to a religious practice. "Stand fast therefore in the liberty by which Christ has made us free, and do not be entangled again with a yoke of bondage" (Gal. 5:1). The bondage that Paul was referring to is the bondage of religious practices or traditions. At the time of that writing, people in Galatia were being told that they had to be circumcised and follow all the Jewish laws to be Christians. That is the very thing that Jesus died to free us from. "Are you so foolish?

Having begun in the Spirit, are you being made perfect by the flesh?" (Gal. 3:3).

It is a good thing to obey the law. It is a good thing to honor the Ten Commandments (and all the others). It is good to try to live right, but don't think that that entitles us to something special. "Christ has redeemed us from the curse of the law" (Gal. 3:13). All the things that I have been writing about in this book are fine and dandy things to do. Reading the Bible, praying, giving, serving—they are all good and healthy things to do, but we never gain status or position with God by doing them.

We don't serve to gain favor with God. We serve because we have gained favor with God. I don't do nice things for my wife in hopes that she will, in turn, love me. I do nice things for my wife because she loves me, and I love her. Love is the motive and not a desire to advance my position. "For we are His workmanship, created in Christ Jesus for good works, which God prepared beforehand that we should walk in them" (Eph. 2:10). We are no accident. We have each been created with skills and abilities to do things. We don't earn extra credit for doing them. Nobody applauds fish for how well they can swim—it's just what they do.

"For if I preach the gospel, I have nothing to boast of, for necessity is laid upon me; yes, woe is me if I do not preach the gospel!" (1 Cor. 9:16). Paul is highly regarded as an apostle. He wrote most of the New Testament epistles. He gave his life in service to the church. He was more committed than most. Yet he didn't think he was worthy of any special consideration for that. He said, "Woe is to me if I do not..."

God is not *moved* by what we do. He is not *moved* by our faith. Who do we think we are that we could *move* God? After He did His work, He sat down. His work was done. Everything we need has been provided. We earnestly desire to find our purpose and fulfill it because there is great benefit for someone else if we do. We have already received the greatest blessing of all—God's favor. We received that by grace through faith in Jesus. There is nothing more to be accomplished.

"For it is by free grace (God's unmerited favor) that you are saved (delivered from judgment and made partakers of Christ's salvation) through (your) faith. And this (salvation) is not of yourselves (of your own doing, it came not through your own striving), but it is the gift of God. Not because of works (not the fulfillment of the law's demands), lest any man should boast. (It is not the result of what anyone can possibly do. So no one can pride himself in it or take glory to himself)" (Eph. 2:8–9 AMP).

"Then God blessed them, and God said to them, 'Be fruitful and multiply'" (Gen. 1:26). Adam and Eve didn't do anything to receive that blessing. God had just created a paradise to sustain them and for them to enjoy. It is the same for us. We are blessed. We are to be fruitful. We may not deserve His mercy. We may not deserve a blessing like that, but this is what God wants to do for us. We should never offend Him by trying to earn or deserve what He is trying to give us as a gift.

We read our Bibles, we pray, we worship to have intimate moments with God. Don't let that become merely some religious practice. This is a relationship with someone we love and who loves us. Don't cheapen it by making it some obligatory routine. If we let our expressions of love be restricted to religious practices, we can miss the genuine interaction with the object of that love—Jesus.

Chapter 19

Where Is There?

With any journey, it's only right to consider, "Where are we going?" To know that is the only way we will know when we get there. The journey of a Christian life is a little different in that the journey actually follows the arrival at the destination.

The moment we believe the Gospel and confess Jesus as Lord, we are saved. We are as saved as we'll ever be. We are just as holy and righteous as we will ever be. We have become *one with Christ*. However, unless we die immediately after that, we have a life to live as a Christian. That life is our journey. The challenges and blessings that follow are what make for a satisfying life.

First of all, relax. So often when Jesus would come onto a scene, He would say, "Peace to you" (Luke 24:36 and many others). There is nothing to accomplish or achieve other than to live a life of value and purpose. It is as if we have been elected to a public office for life. We no longer have to campaign for reelection. We can simply focus on how we can best satisfy the duties of that office. We are well aware of our own personal shortcomings. We would never expect for there to be a statue of us erected in the town square. However, we do want our term in office to be as beneficial as possible for our community.

One of the things most difficult to comprehend is God's love for each of us. God is not a god who loves; He is love. Love is who and what God is. It is His nature to love us just as it is the nature of fire to be hot. I would never approach a bonfire and think, "I hope that fire is warm for me like it is for my friends." "God so loved the world that He gave…" (John 3:16). "God is love" (2 John 4:8, 16). "Behold what manner of love the Father has bestowed on us, that we should be called the children of God!" (1 John 3:1).

"But God—so rich is He in His mercy! Because of and in order to satisfy the great and wonderful and intense love with which He loved us" (Eph. 2:4 AMP). "Thou hast created all things and for thy pleasure they are and were created" (Rev. 4:11 KJV). Just as we are, with all our quirks, we are *intensely* loved by God. We were created for His pleasure. God is not a taskmaster with a whip or a teacher ready to grade our papers. He is a loving Father eager to have us jump into His lap and tell Him all about our day at school.

He has entrusted us with the sharing of His love with others. It is as if He sent us out with enough lunch money for all the kids at school, because He loves them also. That lunch money is not hundreds of pounds of coinage weighing down our pockets. That lunch money is love, joy, peace, and all the other fruits of His Spirit. It is healing, hugs, and compassion that we share with others. The more we give, the more we have. It's one of the great paradoxes of the Christian life. I've heard it said many times by many very different people, "You can't out give God." "And this is His commandment; that we should believe on the name of His Son Jesus Christ and love one another, as He gave us commandment" (1 John 3:23).

The great moments in life are not paying off a mortgage or retiring from a life of labor. The great moments in life are seeing someone healed or delivered or saved. To quote Sam Byrd, a dear old friend, "The greatest thing in life is to be used by God!" Sam was in his midnineties when he said that. If there were *greater things in life*, he would have seen them. We won't necessarily know, at the time, when we are contributing to a great *work of God*. Just as it is God's nature to love, it becomes our nature to give. These moments won't be calculated gestures but simply what we knew to be the right thing to do at the time. We have been given much, so we give much.

The concept of religious practice vanishes, and the concept of a relationship with a loving Father takes its place. We become conduits of His love and experience the joy of His intense love flowing through us. We read the Bible, we pray, we serve at church, we give, we do all sorts of things, but not to achieve something but because of that relationship. As we realize more and more that Jesus' work on the cross is finished, we enter into a rest. We stop trying to *make* good things happen. Instead we simply *let* good things happen. We offer ourselves to be His hands on this earth.

There is no way for our natural minds to begin to comprehend the glories of heaven. God could not even allow Moses to see His face. "You cannot see my face; for no man shall see Me and live" (Exo. 33:20). We read about the streets in heaven paved with gold so pure that it is clear as glass. The foundations of the walls are made of what we here consider to be precious gemstones. I get excited thinking about what the music will be like. When no longer bound by the limitations of our flesh bodies, the sights, sounds, flavors, and other sensations must be exhilarating. For us to experience just a moment of that, I think our natural heads would burst. Fortunately, we won't have these bodies then. "We shall all be changed" (1 Cor. 15:50).

Heaven is our destination, but this life is the journey. It doesn't matter where we start from. The journey, once begun, just gets better and better. Sometimes the road is rocky and the grade steep. We encounter all sorts of weather along the way. But the joy and satisfaction we experience can increase along the way as well. As we mature as Christians, we simply become more effective at letting God's love flow through us. We become less, and He becomes more.

Great athletes work out and practice constantly. I recall reading about Walter Payton running up and down the grandstands at Soldier Field to stay *in shape*. He was already perhaps the greatest football player ever, but he was trying to be better. I am more familiar with musicians who work and practice to be better. The more we play and the more we listen to others, the more we become aware of our own limitations and the harder we work to overcome them. When we get around other musicians and play together, we'll often think about their skill and wish we could do that. Truth be told, oftentimes they are thinking the same thing about us.

Who we are and what we can do becomes small compared to Who is in us and what He wants to do. Whatever skills, talents, abilities, or interests we have were woven into our beings for a purpose. Are we using them? Has our natural self-serving nature been changed by the love of God? Do we spend more time praying for others than we do for ourselves? The journey has begun. We're there! Keep going.

Chapter 20

Persecution

"In the world, you will have tribulation; but be of good cheer, I have overcome the world" (John 16:33). This is not my favorite promise from the Lord. We will have tribulation or trouble. We will have problems, and we will experience persecution. The upside is that He has overcome this world for us, and we should have peace and even joy in the midst of these circumstances.

Here is that whole verse from the Amplified Bible, "I have told you these things, so that in Me you may have (perfect) peace and confidence. In the world, you have tribulation and trials and distress and frustration; but be of good cheer (take courage; be confident, certain, undaunted)! For I have overcome the world. (I have deprived it of its power to harm you and have conquered it for you)" (John 16:33 AMP). This is what Jesus told His disciples the night that He was betrayed, and it applies to us also.

Earlier that night, He said this, "If the world hates you, you know that it hated Me before it hated you" (John 15:18). What have I signed up for?! Now the world hates me? I have to live here; what do I do now? According to Jesus, we are to be of good cheer and be confident and undaunted. "My brethren, count it all joy when you fall into various trials, knowing that the testing of your faith produces patience" (James 1:2–3). When James says *testing*, he does not mean just to see if we have any. He means testing, like strengthening or perfecting our faith. "But let patience have its perfect work, that you may be perfect and complete, lacking nothing" (James 1:4).

When Jesus had that conversation with Nicodemus—the one where that famous John 3:16 verse came from—He said this, "For God did not send His Son into the world to condemn the world, but that the world through Him might be saved. He who believes in Him is not condemned; but he who does not believe is condemned already, because he has not believed in the name of the only begotten Son of God. And this is the condemnation, that the light has come into the world, and men loved darkness rather than light, because their deeds were evil. For everyone practicing evil hates the light and does not come to the light, lest his deeds should be exposed. But he who does the truth comes to the light, that his deeds may be clearly seen, that they have been done in God" (John 3:17–21).

"An unjust man is an abomination to the righteous, and he who is upright in the way is an abomination to the wicked" (Prov. 29:27). If we are righteous in God's eyes, we become an abomination, or something utterly disgusting in the eyes of the wicked or secular world. Some people will think that we have become some vile or icky thing. I have seen people lose friends over this. People who like to party like I used to have an inherent distrust for people who won't get drunk or get high with them.

As a rule, criminals are not friends with cops. People who cheat in sports are not friends with referees or umpires. People who cheat on their tax statements are not friends with IRS auditors. Speeders are not friends with highway patrolmen. Running backs are not friends with linebackers. Get the picture? We have *seen the light* so to speak. We have heard the Gospel and accepted the wonderful gift of salvation. We believe the Bible and accept it as truth—the Word of God. We no longer carry the shame and guilt that the rest of the world still does. We have confidence where they have doubt or fear. We have love, joy, and peace; they only have cheap imitations. We have the power of God working in and through us; they just have their own strength. We have peace with God; the world is at odds with Him. When the world sees that we are different, they don't trust us. They are envious (even if they don't realize that).

ARE WE THERE YET?

We read in Acts chapter 3 that right after the Day of Pentecost, Peter and John went to the temple in Jerusalem. They met a lame man and healed him. When asked how they did it, they simply said it was by the name of Jesus. This got them into all sorts of trouble. As they continued, they were not only threatened, but they were beaten and put in jail. All through the book of Acts, we see this same scenario play out—ordinary people doing mighty works through the name of Jesus and the religious leaders objecting. The early church suffered a great deal of persecution. Most of Paul's epistles were written from prison.

Throughout history, Christians have suffered persecution. To this day, people are being killed for confessing Jesus as Lord. I don't want to get political here, but in many Middle Eastern countries, it is commonplace for Christians to be beheaded. Here in America, we're not likely to be beheaded, but we suffer in other ways. Even though the First Amendment to the US Constitution says, "Congress shall make no law respecting an establishment of religion or prohibiting the free exercise thereof." We are constantly having those rights threatened by civil regulations about nativity scenes or other representations of our faith.

The darkness of this world does not like the light that is in us. By accepting the gift of the grace of God through faith in Jesus, I did not declare that I hate anyone. As a matter of fact, I have assumed a profound love for all people. "For you were once darkness, but now you are light in the Lord. Walk as children of light" (Eph. 5:8). Unsaved people will ask me, "Why do you think you are so special?" I'm not. Jesus is and I'm in Him. When they know my past, they think I'm a hypocrite or even a liar to think I have righteousness. They just don't understand yet. But they are wary of me and see me as an enemy. They become defensive and see my faith as something that is against them personally.

Jesus said, "If you were of the world, the world would love its own. Yet because you are not of the world, but I chose you out of the world, therefore the world hates you. Remember the word that I said to you, 'A servant is not greater than his master.' If they persecuted Me, they will also persecute you. If they kept My word, they will keep yours also. But all these things they will do to you for My name's sake, because they do not know Him who sent Me. If I had not come and spoken to them, they would have no sin, but now they have no excuse for their sin. He who hates Me hates My Father also. If I had not done among them the works which no one else did, they would have no sin; but now they have seen and also hated both Me and My Father. But this happened that the word might be fulfilled which is written in their law, 'They hated Me without a cause'" (John 15:19–25).

The world's hatred of Jesus, of God, and of us is *without cause*. But the world's hatred is still there. "The thief does not come except to steal and to kill and to destroy. I have come that they may have life and that they may have it more abundantly" (John 10:10). All Jesus wants to do is save people from destruction, and that is now our mission also. It seems a noble cause to me, and not something that we should be hated for. But there is an enemy—*the thief,* as Jesus put it. Since the days of Adam and Eve (and their sin), the world has been under the sway of the wicked one, the devil. It is his desire that we all die. God is love. Guess what the devil is full of.

If people were inside a building and looked out the window to see us standing in the rain, they think we're silly or stupid. If they knew that their building was on fire, they'd have a different attitude. The world is bound by secular philosophies, traditions of man, and primal urges. They don't know their building is on fire. They just see us as different. They think we are just being self-righteous. They don't know that there is real righteousness available to all people through Jesus.

Don't be alarmed or discouraged by their response to us. The love that we share is alien to them. Love anyway. The fact that we are Christians makes them think we are judging them. We are not; just love them. They will experience conviction from the Holy Spirit, just like we did. This might make them feel uncomfortable. They will think we are making them uncomfortable. We are not; just love them. They may even want to put us in jail or cut off our heads. Just love them.

"In the world, you will have tribulation; but be of good cheer, I have overcome the world" (John 16:33).

Chapter 21

Keep It Simple

As we learn more and more about what the Bible says, we gain an opportunity to become a little conceited about our own depth of knowledge. I caution against that. Keep it simple and stay humble. The Word is our teacher, and we are the students, and that relationship will never change.

"For I determined not to know anything among you except Jesus Christ and Him crucified" (1 Cor. 2:2). It is good to be constantly learning and growing in the faith. "Grace and peace be multiplied to you in the knowledge of God and of Jesus, our Lord" (2 Pet. 1:2). To grow in knowledge is to grow in *grace and peace*.

We will find that other people will have a different understanding about some things. Different churches have specific belief systems regarding various points of theology. And these differences have led to arguments between brothers in the faith. I would caution anyone to not get overly caught up in denominational doctrines. Look at everything through gospel-colored glasses. Anytime someone says, "I don't find anything in the Bible that supports that belief." It may mean that they just haven't found it yet or maybe it isn't there. But when scripture is found that supports a belief, then we have something; especially if we find two or three examples.

As we read through the Gospels, we see very many times where people would approach Jesus wanting to be healed. These people were not Christians. They were mostly Jews who were under the Old

Covenant of the law. All they knew was that this Jesus person healed people. They had heard the reports and wanted to give Him a try. No deep theology here; they just knew that the miraculous power of God was with Him.

That Gospel is simple. "For God so loved the world that He gave His only begotten Son that whosoever believes on Him shall not perish but have everlasting life" (John 3:16). "For by grace you have been saved through faith" (Eph. 2:8). "That if you confess with your mouth the Lord Jesus and believe in your heart that God raised Him from the dead, you will be saved" (Rom. 10:9). God makes it simple. We tend to complicate things.

"Stand fast therefore in the liberty by which Christ has made us free, and do not be entangled again with a yoke of bondage" (Gal. 5:1). Paul was warning us to not fall back into a system of bondage to a long list of dos and don'ts. We are to love and not judge people. Beyond that it is just a matter of maturing in the faith and gaining greater control over our own natural tendencies—our flesh.

Paul compares the things of the flesh with the things of the Spirit. "Now the works of the flesh are evident, which are adultery, fornication, uncleanness, lewdness, idolatry, sorcery, hatred, contentions, jealousies, outbursts of wrath, selfish ambitions, dissensions, heresies, envy, murders, drunkenness, revelries, and the like" (Gal. 5:19–21). This is not a list of capital crimes for believers. These are the things that our flesh (and I mean all of us), by nature, tends to want to do.

"But the fruit of the Spirit is love, joy, peace, long-suffering, kindness, goodness, faithfulness, gentleness, and self-control" (Gal. 5:22–23). "For those who live according to the flesh set their minds on the things of the flesh, but those who live according to the Spirit, the things of the Spirit" (Rom. 8:5). We need to be careful what we *set our minds on*. The good news that God loves us, and what Jesus did on the cross for us, and that He is risen from the grave are the things we should set our minds on. And the fact that we have been given this wonderful gift by a gracious and loving God is reason enough to want to share it with others.

"And I, brethren, when I came to you, did not come with excellence of speech or of wisdom declaring to you the testimony of God. For I determined not to know anything among you except Jesus Christ and Him crucified. I was with you in weakness, in fear, and in much trembling. And my speech and my preaching were not with persuasive words of human wisdom, but in demonstration of the Spirit and of power, that your faith should not be in the wisdom of men but in the power of God" (1 Cor. 2:1–5). As we grow in knowledge and understanding, we should also grow in the wisdom to keep the simple and fundamental things of the Gospel first and foremost in our thoughts and in our words.

It is good news! It is free—that's what *gift* means. It was given to us, and we can share it with others. If we realize that someone does not know Jesus, it should break our hearts that they are needlessly suffering through an empty life. With a heart of compassion, we should want them to have the blessings of God like we do. Pointing to the law and pointing to their shortcomings will not gain an entry to their heart. The more we step back and let God pour through us the better. Love, joy, peace, kindness, gentleness, and generosity will draw people to a saving knowledge of Jesus. We all have a testimony. We can all share how we are not what we used to be and how wonderful it is to just know Jesus. But keep it simple.

CHAPTER 22

One Day We'll Know

I have always known that there are very many different denominations of Christian churches. I never knew exactly why, and to some degree, I still don't, nor do I really care. There are Baptist churches, Methodist churches, and so on and so on. I remember seeing a sign that mentioned, "First Baptist Church," and in my ignorance I thought, "Wow! That was the first one."

On the day of Pentecost, considered to be the birth of the New Testament church, there were no such distinctions—only *the Church*. The Church (with a capital C) would be the body of believers. In other words, all the people of the world who believe in Jesus, confess Him as Lord, and believe that God raised Him from the dead (Rom. 10:9–10).

Since then there have been many groups who think that they are the *real* church to the exclusion of other believers. There has been the Catholic Church—of which there are now the Roman Catholic, Greek Orthodox, and Russian Orthodox. Then, there was the Protestant reformation. And now there are many different Protestant denominations or schools of doctrinal philosophy. It can present the opportunity to raise needless division among believers. To put all these differences into perspective, I would like to share an experience I had many years ago.

I had not been a believer for but maybe a year, and I was enthusiastic about my newfound faith. I was working at a paint store at the time. One day, at lunch time, I was sitting in the store's little break room reading my Bible when a coworker came in. He saw that I was reading, and he asked, "What are you reading?" To which I replied, "Revelation."

"Oh," he said and then he went on to say that his church, "did not believe in a secret rapture of the church." My mind immediately thought of Paul's description of such an event from 1 Thessalonians 4:16–17. I was ready to argue the point.

Then he said these magic words, "I guess one day we'll know." Pow! Just like that, our differences vanished and were replaced with what we have in common. He was a Christian. I was a Christian. We went to different churches that had some differences in opinion about certain things. But those differences became instantly small compared to what we had in common—Jesus.

I've heard it said that "In the fundamentals of the faith, we have unity. In the nonfundamentals of the faith, we have liberty. And in all things, we have love." Those are golden words. Battle lines can be drawn over so many things, but we don't have to engage in a battle with anyone. Whether baptism means sprinkled or dunked; whether communion should be with wine or grape juice; whether or not there should be drums or guitars in a worship service—the list goes on forever it seems. It is a ploy of our common enemy, the devil, to introduce division.

Anyone who is a believer needs to attend church regularly. We are not meant to walk alone. Churches provide, support, accountability, and opportunities to serve. Just make sure that the Bible is the foundation of the teaching there. We commit to the church we attend, but this is not a marriage. If we find that what is taught is in direct conflict with what the Bible says, we may need to find a different church—pray about that. Sometimes God will direct us to go to a different church. It does not mean that one is good and another is bad. It just means that what God wants to do through us is needed somewhere else. I would advise any new believer to faithfully attend church and get involved.

Some of the things that I have written about in this book are not shared in some churches. Please don't let that be a problem. What we all have in common, as believers, is Jesus and the Word. Study the Word, feed on the Word, pray, worship, give, and be led by the Holy Spirit. When division presents itself, recognize it as a ploy of the devil to introduce doubt. I am, by no means, the Bible know-it-all. I am simply here to help any new believer get going toward his own calling and the maturity and usefulness that God has created for him. Be blessed. Be fruitful and multiply.

APPENDIX

The Sacraments—Baptism and Communion

Baptism

Once a person has accepted Jesus Christ as Lord, there is a common practice called baptism. This is simply a very public demonstration of a person's newfound faith. It is by no means a requirement for salvation, but it is a good thing to do with plenty of scriptural precedent.

There was a fellow named John the Baptist who baptized people in the Jordan River. People would come down into the river with John, and he would dunk them under the water. This was a ceremonial expression of that person's commitment to following God. Three of the Gospels describe John baptizing Jesus (Matt. 3:13–17; Mark 1:9–11; and Luke 3:21–22).

There is a verse that had me a little confused when I first heard it. "He who believes and is baptized will be saved" (Mark 16:16). This sounded like a checklist. So as a youngster, not really knowing anything about what I was doing, I got baptized thinking that I was fulfilling some sort of required thing to do or accomplish. After all, I didn't want to go to hell. If this is all I had to do, I'm covered now. I have learned a lot since then, and I'd like to share.

When Jesus died on the cross, they put His body in a tomb. Three days later, He rose from that grave and is alive forevermore. When we get baptized, it symbolizes our own death and resurrection in Christ. Paul puts it this way, "Or do you not know that as many of us as were baptized into Christ Jesus were baptized into His death? Therefore we were buried with Him through baptism into death, that just as Christ was raised from the dead by the glory of the Father, even so we also should walk in newness of life" (Rom. 6:3–4). "Likewise you also, reckon yourselves to be dead indeed to sin, but alive to God in Christ Jesus our Lord" (Rom. 6:11).

Baptism is mentioned often in the Gospels, Acts, and the epistles. It is a good thing to do. It is a public confession of our faith in Jesus. But it is by no means a requirement for salvation. A guilty and condemned man that hung on a cross next to Jesus said something to Jesus. He said, "Lord, remember me when You come into Your kingdom" (Luke 23:42). To which Jesus replied, "Assuredly, I say to you, today you will be with Me in Paradise" (Luke 23:43). He called Jesus Lord, and Jesus said that he'd be with Jesus in Paradise. There is no record of this man ever getting baptized—he was nailed to a cross when his attitude changed.

It is a humbling thing to be submerged under water in front of people. It is very indiscreet to be completely wet and not because we are swimming or bathing. It is a public confession of our faith in Jesus, and that we are now a new creature in Christ. Jesus said, "Whoever confesses Me before men, him I will confess before My Father who is in heaven," (Matt. 10:32). This is such a confession.

Some churches dunk and some churches sprinkle. Don't let that confuse or be a distraction from what is really going on. I don't know where the tradition of sprinkling came about, but it is still a public confession of faith in Jesus. Some churches will even bless the water and call it holy water, but it is just water. It is symbolism and ceremony. As that youngster, when I wanted to get baptized to satisfy what I thought was a requirement, I was sprinkled. Many years later, when I actually knew something about what this was all about, I was dunked. This was simply a reflection of what the two different churches I had attended used as their convention of baptism—it's a matter of style.

Communion

Another thing that we will experience when we start going to church is something called communion (sometimes referred to as the Eucharist). It involves eating bread, usually crackers of some sort, and drinking some wine, often just grape juice. Like baptism, this is a symbolic gesture. It is a religious rite or practice, but it can have a profoundly positive benefit.

To the uninformed, it may seem like minimal refreshments. But once we understand the symbolism, this can have a deep, very personal, physical, and spiritual impact. Jesus explains it this way, "And He took bread, gave thanks and broke it, and gave it to them, saying, 'This is My body which is given for you; do this in remembrance of Me.' Likewise He also took the cup after supper, saying, 'This cup is the new covenant in My blood, which is shed for you'" (Luke 22:19–20). He had not gone to the cross yet when He did this. So obviously this was a symbolic gesture.

Paul restates this with this explanation, "The Lord Jesus on the same night in which He was betrayed took bread; and when He had given thanks, He broke it and said, 'Take, eat; this is My body which is broken for you. Do this in remembrance of Me.' In the same manner, He also took the cup after supper, saying, 'This cup is the New Covenant in My blood. This do as often as you drink it, in remembrance of Me.' For as often as you eat this bread and drink this cup, you proclaim the Lord's death till He comes" (1 Cor. 11:23–26).

That's about as deep as it gets in most church services—a solemn and somber moment, a little wine or juice and a little cracker, and we remember Jesus. But it can be so much more. When we remember the fact that Jesus was beaten, brutalized, and nailed to a cross, we are reminded of why He did that. Isaiah prophesized about these hundreds of years before it took place. "Surely, He has borne our griefs and carried our sorrows; yet we esteemed Him stricken, smitten by God, and afflicted. But He was wounded for our transgressions, He was bruised for our iniquities; the chastisement for our peace was upon Him, and by His stripes we are healed" (Is. 53:4–5).

There is two parts to what Jesus, Paul, and Isaiah are speaking of here. They are symbolized by the bread and the wine. The bread, the body of Jesus, was broken. He suffered a great deal of abuse at the hands of Roman soldiers. He was also beaten with whips that left stripes on His back. Those stripes, that abuse, and ultimately

His death on the cross was for our healing. And that blood ratified the New Covenant of grace, which redeemed us from the curse of the law. This is what we are to remember when we partake of the communion.

Peter reminds us of this also, speaking of Jesus on the Cross, "Who when He was reviled, did not revile in return; when He suffered, He did not threaten, but committed Himself to Him who judges righteously; who Himself bore our sins in His own body on the tree, that we having died to sins, might live for righteousness—by whose stripes you were healed" (1 Pet. 2:23–24). The entirety of the Gospel is symbolized by this one ceremony. Jesus bore, in His own body, all the sin of mankind—that includes ours. And He also bore our sickness and disease.

This is a great moment to really take to heart the truth of what Jesus did for us. Friends, doctors, or even symptoms might be telling us that we are sick, but when we remember Jesus on the cross, we realize that we are healed. This requires the faith to cling to a truth, even if it contradicts what we think we see or hear. This is what Paul speaks of as discerning the Lord's body. "For he who eats and drinks in an unworthy manner eats and drinks judgment on himself, not discerning the Lord's body. For this reason many are weak and sick among you" (1 Cor. 11:20–30). Many are weak or sick because they fail to discern the Lord's body—they fail to really believe and embrace the fact that by His stripes we are healed. Some people refer to this as the meal that heals.

When we partake of the communion meal, we also are reminded of the wonderful grace of God; that all our sins are forgiven, and we are free from the curse or consequences of the law. Jesus was the sacrificial Lamb, whose blood paid the price for all that once and for all (Rom. 6:10; Heb. 10:10). "It is finished" (John 19:30). There is nothing for us to do but accept this wonderful gift from God. We have been shown great grace and mercy. We should now go and do likewise by being gracious and merciful.

When we bite into that bread or cracker, we remember what was done to Jesus, and we discern that it was for our healing. When we drink that wine or juice, we remember that Jesus shed His blood to pay for our sins and usher us into the kingdom of His Father's love. What is our response? We are extremely grateful. We give thanks. And we can do this anywhere and anytime. I have done this at a Burger King with a whopper and a coke. It's all in the remembrance. This is a great time to come back to the simple truth of the Gospel and fully embrace all what God wants for us.

The Roman's Road

Rom 3:10—There is none righteous, no not one.
Rom 3:23—For all have sinned and fall short of the glory of God.
Rom 5:12—Through one man sin entered the world, and death through sin, and thus death spread to all men, because all sinned.
Rom 6:23—For the wages of sin is death, but the gift of God is eternal life in Christ Jesus our Lord.
Rom 5:8—But God demonstrates His own love toward us, in that while we were still sinners, Christ died for us.
Rom 10:13—For whoever calls on the name of the Lord shall be saved.
Rom 10:9–10—That if you confess with your mouth the Lord Jesus and believe in you heart that God has raised Him from the dead, you will be saved. For with the heart one believes unto righteousness and with the mouth confession is made unto salvation.

Emergency Numbers

When in sorrow	Call John 14
When men fail you	Call Psalm 27
When you want to be fruitful	Call John 15
When you have sinned	Call Psalm 51
When you worry	Call Matthew 6:19–34
You are in danger	Call Psalm 91
When God seems far away	Call Psalm 139

When your faith needs stirring	Call Hebrews 11
When you are lonely and fearful	Call Psalm 23
When you grow bitter and critical	Call 1 Corinthians 13
For Paul's secret of happiness	Call 1 Cor. 3:12–17
For Paul's idea of Christianity	Call 1 Cor. 5:15–19
When you feel down and out	Call Romans 8:31–39
When you want rest and peace	Call Matthew 11:25–30
When the world seems bigger than God	Call Psalm 70
When you want Christian assurance	Call Romans 8:1–30
When you leave home for labor or travel	Call Psalm 121
When your prayers grow narrow or selfish	Call Psalm 67

Time and chronology

In my youth, I was a student of science. In high school, higher math, chemistry, biology, and physics classes helped me keep my grade point average up because they were interesting enough to maintain my attention. This led to college where I studied chemistry and engineering.

I loved the concept of science in its purity. It was a process of challenging long held beliefs through testing and observation. Its purpose was to discover a better understanding of truth or what really is. "Is the earth flat?" might have been a question. "Let's test that" would be a response. After Magellan circumnavigated the earth, and especially since we now have photos from space that show that the earth is spherical in nature, we conclude that the earth is not flat. This is science in its pure form.

Unfortunately our colleges and universities have become, to a large extent, the kind of institution that science originally was designed to challenge. Even in the fields of science, they have their traditional sacred concepts like evolution and a big bang theory that have become their religious dogma. And we dare not challenge them—at least if we want to pass their course and get that degree.

One of those sacred concepts is that the earth is very, very old. Somehow scientists have calculated that the earth is millions or billions of years old. It seems to me that this age thing is a smokescreen to cover the fact that their ideas about how it all came to pass are unlikely without it taking a remarkably long period of time. It seems that all their models begin with the same assumption that the Bible is a work of fiction and not a historical document. (I use the word *model* instead of *theory* here because they don't qualify as a theory according to scientific process.)

When I was a student, I went along with their concepts. After all, they were university professors with PhDs and other degrees and credentials. But in the back of my mind lingered doubts. These things didn't really make sense to me, and from a purely scientific perspective, I wrestled with them. I remember seeing news reports about huge mudslides that happened in the mountains after a large rainstorm. The thrust of their story was that Highway 50 was closed due to a mudslide, but I wondered how much dirt would have had to be up there for millions or billions of storms to have happened like that, and yet the mountains were still there and there was still enough dirt left to close a highway.

Almost twenty years later, something happened that changed my perspective on these things. I met Jesus! I also heard God say to me, "Read My Word!" This may seem spooky to some people, but it really did happen, and I knew it was God. (I knew that neither the devil nor my own imagination would tell me to read the Bible.) This changed my perspective on a great many things. Now I started with the assumption that, "Every word of God is pure" (Prov. 30:5). Now I had what I now consider as truth against which I can measure those scientific concepts that I used to doubt.

One of those concepts is the old age of the earth. I started in Genesis and added up the years of Adam's age when Seth was born with the age of Seth when Enosh was born and so on. I found that the flood happened around sixteen hundred years or so after the days of creation. I also continued this process using biblical timeframes up to the time of the Babylonian captivity and from there I used other historical references.

Oh my! According to the Bible, the earth is about six thousand years old. That flood had some pretty devastating impact on the earth that makes a lot more sense to me than the stories that the modern scientists make up. Also, from a prophetic standpoint, that age could suggest that an end is near, but that's a whole different story. Prophecy has not been my focus of study. But I do want to point out a very significant thing about this model of the earth's age that is relevant to us right now.

For the sake of simpler math, I made up a term that I call the *useful lifespan of a person*. I figure that from the time a person matures to a point of usefulness until they are too old to continue in that capacity to be about sixty years. (Again, this is just to make the math easy—people can certainly be useful much longer than that.) If we divide sixty years by a million or a billion, the useful lifespan of a person is totally insignificant. We are nothing but dust in the wind – just a tiny speck too small to measure. However, if we consider the age of the earth as six thousand years, that useful lifespan equals 1 percent of the total of human existence. Now all of a sudden, we are significant!

Think about it. If our milk carton was 1 percent bad, would we put it on our cereal? If we had a 1 percent chance of crashing, would we take that flight or just drive? If we were on a submarine, would we be satisfied with 99 percent hull integrity? One percent now matters.

If we were in a room with one hundred people and one of them was Shaquille O'Neal, wouldn't we probably spot him pretty quickly? If we were part of a taskforce of one hundred people, and one of them was Donald Trump, how long would it take for him to emerge? In a rock band with one hundred musicians, I believe we'd know it if Jimi Hendrix was there.

The bottom line is that we all are significant parts of the history of mankind. Our lives and the impact we have on humanity is not the insignificant thing that the so-called scientists would like to suggest. Every one of us can make our mark on the history of man. Every famous person in history had a life, and we do too. When I was born, there were people still alive who were around during the Civil War. I remember an old relative telling me about being in the earthquake in San Francisco (I mean the one in the early twentieth century). Our lives span more of history than we typically realize.

We dare not let anyone lead us to think that our lives do not matter. We can waste it, but the potential is there to have a real impact. We must find our God-given purpose, make our mark, and have our impact. If there were only one hundred pages in the history book of mankind, our lives would cover one of those pages! Make sure something great is written there.

Bible Overview

The Bible, as we know it, consists of sixty-six books. There are thirty-nine books in what we call the Old Testament, and twenty-seven books in what we call the New Testament. There are many other writings from that period of, but these are what is commonly considered to be the Bible.

The first five books of the Bible are referred to as the Pentateuch. Moses is considered to be the author. (When I say *author*, I really mean the one who wrote down the words as they were given to him by God.) These writings cover a couple thousand years of human history as well as the birth and development of the nation of Israel.

What follows is twelve books that describe approximately another thousand years of the history of the nation of Israel. There was a period of time when Israel was led by judges. And then there was a period where they were led by kings. After Solomon's reign, the nation was divided into two kingdoms. Both kingdoms eventually were taken into captivity by other nations. Finally, the kingdom was restored.

After the historical accounts comes the poetic books. These books contain history, prophecy, and some profoundly succinct wisdom. The nature of these writings is unique among the scriptures. Job is a most unusual account of one man's life. The Psalms is literally a book of songs. The Proverbs is nuggets of wisdom laid out in a devotional fashion. And Ecclesiastes and Song of Solomon give perspective on human wisdom and love.

The books of the prophets come next. Isaiah, Jeremiah, Ezekiel, and Daniel are considered to be the major prophets simply because their writings are of greater volume. The rest of the seventeen prophetic books are the works of the minor prophets. Again these are considered as such simply because of their writing's relative brevity.

For about four hundred years, there were no more prophetic writings. Then came the birth of Jesus! The first four books of the New Testament are what is referred to as the Gospels. Matthew, Mark, Luke, and John each document the life, ministry, and sayings of Jesus. Matthew and John actually were of the original disciples of Jesus, but all four accounts are the inspired Word of God.

Immediately following the Gospels is the book of Acts, or the Acts of the Apostles. The Acts is a continuation of Luke's Gospel and is a historical account of the early church and the ministry of Paul and other apostles.

The New Testament contains twenty-one epistles or letters. Thirteen of these epistles were written by Paul. It is not certain who wrote the book of Hebrews. James wrote a letter, as did Jude. Peter wrote two and John wrote three. These were all letters written to encourage and teach the early churches that were springing up in many different areas. In some cases, they were written to a specific church, but they were all intended to be passed around and read by all.

Finally, there is the Revelation of Jesus Christ. This is the grand prophetic climax to the Bible. Many of the Old Testament prophecies have already been fulfilled—most of them relate to the nation of Israel or the birth, life, death, and resurrection of Jesus. Revelation contains a lot of prophecy about things that have not yet happened but are perhaps beginning to happen in our lifetime.

The order of the books in the Old Testament is not entirely chronological either by subject or writing. The same is somewhat true about the order of the books in the New Testament. The overarching theme throughout scripture is the love, grace, and mercy of God, as well as His supreme authority and power. The redemptive work of Jesus is reflected throughout scripture as well. The Bible is like a string of sixty-six beautiful pearls on a necklace. I like to think that a day will come when we will all have perfect knowledge, and it will be like seeing down that string and seeing Jesus as the common thread throughout all of it.

"Grace and peace be multiplied to you in the knowledge of God and of Jesus our Lord" (2 Pet. 1:2). It is not just knowledge about God and Jesus our Lord. It is knowledge of Him. It is a personal relationship with Jesus. I think of the Bible as a love letter written from Jesus to us. "I go to prepare a place for you" (John 14:2). Jesus ascended to heaven, sent the Holy Spirit, our Helper, to help us live the life we are called to, and the Bible is a great help to guide us on our journey.

Book	Subject	Author	Approximate Date
Old Testament			
Genesis	"In the beginning" is how this book starts, and this is the theme of this book. The creation of the universe, the creation and fall of man, Noah and the flood, and the generations that lead to Abraham and his descendants are all detailed here.	Moses	1500 BC
Exodus	The descendants of Abraham, what would become the nation of Israel had been in captivity in Egypt. This is the story of their deliverance led by Moses. Here we will also see the introduction of "The Old Covenant of the Law."	Moses	1500 BC
Leviticus	This is a detailed list of specific laws and procedures of the law. These things cover civil and moral matters as well as ceremonial and practical matters as well.	Moses	1500 BC

Numbers	The wanderings of the nation of Israel are documented here. They were in the desert for forty years and experienced many dramatic things.	Moses	1500 BC
Deuteronomy	Moses was 120 years old and about to die, so he put all the matters of the law in order. Here we also have the blessings and the curses of the law.	Moses	1500 BC
Joshua	The baton of leadership had been passed from Moses to Joshua. Now they are going into the Promised Land to take possession starting with Jericho.	perhaps Joshua	1400 BC
Judges	After Joshua dies there follows a period of about three hundred years in which the people of the twelve tribes of Israel are led by a series of Judges. Here is where we read about Samson, Gideon, Deborah, and others. Israel was constantly falling away from God and constantly delivered from enemies.	perhaps Samuel	1100 BC
Ruth	One of two books of the Bible where a woman is the central character. Ruth eventually became the great-grandmother of David. This is a lovely story of redemption.	perhaps Samuel	1100 BC
1 Samuel	Samuel was the last judge of the series that began in the book of Judges. Samuel was also a prophet. Here we have records of Saul becoming the first king of Israel. We also have an account of David fighting Goliath and later becoming the King.	perhaps Samuel	1100 BC

2 Samuel	David is finally made the king and Jerusalem becomes the capitol of the kingdom; 2 Samuel details the times of David's reign as king.	perhaps Samuel	1050 BC
1 Kings	After David's death, Solomon became king of Israel, and the temple is built. Then after Solomon's death, the kingdom is divided into the northern kingdom (Israel) and southern kingdom (Judah).	perhaps Jeremiah	600 BC
2 Kings	This is a continuation of 1 Kings detailing the reigns of subsequent kings of both kingdoms and their troubles—ultimately their capture by Babylon.	perhaps Jeremiah	600 BC
1 Chronicles	This book starts back with Adam and lists the various families or generations leading up to David. It then is a second account of things written of in 1 Kings.	perhaps Ezra	450 BC
2 Chronicles	A continuation of 1 Chronicles, we have now a second account of the reign of Solomon and the subsequent kings of both kingdoms. And we have another account of their captivity by Babylon.	perhaps Ezra	450 BC
Ezra	The nation of Israel was in captivity in Babylon for seventy years. Here we have the return of Israel from captivity and the rebuilding to the temple in Jerusalem.	probably Ezra	450 BC

Nehemiah	This book is a continuation of the book Ezra. This book covers the rebuilding of the wall at Jerusalem and the beginning of the return to the Old Covenant laws and traditions.	probably Ezra	450 BC
Esther	Esther is the other Old Testament book whose central character is a woman. And once again, this is a marvelous story of redemption. Esther was Jewish, yet she became queen of Persia and at just the right time.	perhaps Ezra	450 BC
Job	Some say this is the oldest text of the Bible. It is an unusual story about a man named Job who suffered many things and yet remained faithful to God. Most of the book is dialogue between Job, his wife and a couple friends, and eventually, God Himself.	unknown	900 BC
Psalms	This is known as the book of songs. It's like a Hebrew hymnal. It is the largest book of the Bible by far. Modern music styles such as praise, worship, ballads, and blues are found here. This was all to be set to music; many have instructions for how they are to be played. Psalms contains the longest chapter of any book in the Bible as well as the shortest chapter. Many of the Psalms contain words of prophecy, including some very specific references to Jesus.	David, Moses and perhaps others	1000 to 500 BC

Proverbs	Proverbs is known as the Book of Wisdom. There are thirty-one chapters of succinct nuggets of wisdom that are easy to learn and recall.	mostly Solomon	950 BC
Ecclesiastes	Solomon was one of the wealthiest and most powerful people who ever lived. He was perhaps the wisest man in history. He indulged himself in every earthly pleasure that there was and found that it was "vanity" compared to knowing God.	Solomon	930 BC
Song of Solomon	This is another song—this time a love song. It gets pretty racy at times with rather graphic descriptions of human intimacy. Profound and intense love is described here, and it is a metaphor for the love Jesus has for His bride.	Solomon	950 BC
Isaiah	Isaiah is sometimes referred to as the Messianic prophet. There are sixty-six chapters of this book that offer great warnings about the nation of Israel falling away from God and also prophetic words about the Babylonian captivity and the eventual return of Israel to the Promised Land. This book has unmistakable references to Jesus and was quoted many times in the New Testament.	Isaiah	740 BC
Jeremiah	Jeremiah was known as the weeping prophet. He spent his time warning the people of Jerusalem about Babylon. They didn't listen.	Jeremiah	650 BC

Lamentations	I call this book Jerry Sings the Blues. It is a sad tale of the destruction of Jerusalem. Ironically there is a short passage that is very uplifting: "His mercies are new every morning" (ch. 3, vs. 23).	Jeremiah	560 BC
Ezekiel	Ezekiel lived during the time of the Babylonian captivity. His prophecies often deal with things that are still in the future. It must have been difficult for him to describe visions of helicopters, missiles or the implements of now modern warfare.	Ezekiel	590 BC
Daniel	Daniel and his friends, Shadrach, Meshach, and Abed-Nego, were captive in Babylon, but Daniel had some position there because of his gift of interpreting dreams. Here we have the story of Daniel in the lion's den, the four men in the fire, and some others. There are also some profound prophecies about things that are still to happen.	Daniel	600 BC
Hosea	Hosea was instructed by God to take a wife who was a harlot. This was to show the nation of Israel how they had drifted into spiritual harlotry.	Hosea	740 BC
Joel	Joel's work was a call to repentance for the nation of Judah. There is also a mention of a day when God would "pour out His Spirit." This was quoted by Peter on the day of Pentecost.	Joel	740 BC

ARE WE THERE YET?

Amos	Amos was a farmer turned prophet. He spoke to the nation of Israel about their sinful nature during a time of prosperity.	Amos	740 BC
Obadiah	This is a word against Edom. Edom was the descendants of Esau, and since the days of Jacob and Esau, there was trouble between Edom and Israel.	Obadiah	580 BC
Jonah	This is that great story about Jonah being called to minister to the people of Nineveh. He didn't want to do it and wound up in the belly of a "great fish."	Jonah	780 BC
Micah	Micah was a contemporary of Isaiah and prophesied against the people of Jerusalem.	Micah	740 BC
Naham	Naham prophesied against the nation of Assyria shortly before their destruction.	Naham	610 BC
Habakkuk	"The just shall live by faith" (Hab. 2:4). Habakkuk prophesies against the nation of Judah.	Habakkuk	600 BC
Zephaniah	Zephaniah's prophecies may have had an impact on the brief upturn in the moral compass of Judah during the reign of Josiah.	Zephaniah	620 BC
Haggai	Haggai spoke words of encouragement to the people returning to Jerusalem after the Babylonian captivity.	Haggai	520 BC
Zechariah	God, through Zechariah, encouraged the people of Jerusalem to return to God and also to finish the rebuilding of the temple.	Zechariah	520 BC

Malachi	Malachi spoke of repentance from the sinful ways of the post-exilic Jerusalem, its leaders, and its priests.	probably Malachi	450 BC
NEW TESTAMENT			
Matthew	Matthew (or Levi) was a tax collector and an early disciple of Jesus. This book shows from a Jewish perspective that Jesus is of the lineage of David and is the fulfillment of prophecy as the Messiah.	Matthew	AD 55
Mark	Mark traveled with Peter and also with Paul. The emphasis of Mark's Gospel is the miraculous power that Jesus used.	Mark	AD 65
Luke	Luke, like Mark, was not one of the original apostles, but he traveled with Paul. Luke is the only gentile, or non-Jewish, writer of any of the Bible books. Luke was a physician, and his writing is very detailed and orderly. Here we have to great "Christmas Story" in the first two chapters.	Luke	AD 75
John	John was one of the original disciples. This Gospel opens with, "In the beginning," showing that Jesus, the Word, has always been. There are lots of Jesus' quotes in this Gospel, as well as an extended account of the time in the upper room on the night of His betrayal.	John	AD 80
Acts	This is a continuation of Luke's Gospel, and it describes, in detail, the growth of the early church beginning with the Day of Pentecost in chapter 2.	Luke	AD 62

Romans	This is one of the grandest books, or letters, ever written. Paul thoroughly details the mechanics of salvation as well as great advice for a proper life.	Paul	AD 56
1 Corinthians	Paul digs deep into matters of righteousness and behavior. Here we also have details about the Lord's Supper, gifts of the Holy Spirit and that famous chapter about love (chapter 13).	Paul	AD 55
2 Corinthians	This is a follow-up letter to the church in Corinth. Paul's tone is gentler than in the previous letter, and he defends his role as an apostle.	Paul	AD 56
Galatians	This is a small book in size but huge in its clarity. The Galatians were being told that they had to follow all the Jewish laws to be saved. Paul corrects that very clearly.	Paul	AD 55
Ephesians	Paul's letter to the Ephesians is an excellent follow-up to Galatians. The first two chapters are extremely deep and powerful. Here we have instructions for a proper and victorious Christian life.	Paul	AD 55
Philippians	Here we have great advice for living in peace with God and with people.	Paul	AD 61
Colossians	Paul explains that Jesus Christ is at the center of His church, us, and our lives.	Paul	AD 61
1 Thessalonians	Paul expresses gratitude for a faithful and loving church in Thessalonica. Chapter 4 details the "catching away or rapture of the church."	Paul	AD 50

2 Thessalonians	This is a follow-up letter to the church in Thessalonica. Here we have additional warnings about false teachings.	Paul	AD 50
1 Timothy	Timothy was a young leader in the church at Ephesus. Here Paul gives encouragement and advice about how a leader should lead.	Paul	AD 64
2 Timothy	Shortly before his death, Paul sends another letter to Timothy to encourage him.	Paul	AD 68
Titus	Titus was a young leader of the church in Crete. Here we have instructions about appointing elders to oversee church matters.	Paul	AD 64
Philemon	This is an unusual letter. It wasn't written to a church so much as it was written to a person. But it is useful for all of us. Philemon had a slave named Onesimus who had escaped and met Paul. Paul is asking Philemon to forgive Onesimus and set him free.	Paul	AD 61
Hebrews	This is a glorious explanation of the New Covenant versus the Old Covenant. Contained herein is the famous chapter 11—the "Faith Hall of Fame."	unknown	AD 67
James	Faith without works is dead is the theme here. Those works are actually living a life of love rather than just accepting some matters as truth.	James	AD 50
1 Peter	Peter encourages us to live godly lives in spite of persecution.	Peter	AD 62
2 Peter	Peter encourages us to stand firm in the faith.	Peter	AD 65

1 John	Live in the light and love of God. "God is love" is found in this book twice. This book combats false teaching and reaffirms our commandment to love.	John	AD 90
2 John	This is the shortest book in the New Testament. We are to walk in love and truth and beware of deceivers.	John	AD 90
3 John	This is just a few more warnings and words of encouragement.	John	AD 90
Jude	Jude was a primary leader of the early church in Jerusalem. Here he warns of false teaching.	Jude	AD 65–80
Revelation	This is a revelation of things to come, given to Jesus and shared with John. The imagery and symbolism are a challenge to comprehend. But this is prophecy that describe many events that will definitely take place in the future. Persecution and tribulation ramp up dramatically.	John	AD 90

Rightly Divide

Having read the Bible as many times as I have, there are lots of phrases or expressions that I have heard many times without deep consideration at that time. There are so many things worthy of deep consideration—perhaps every word, but today this expression caught my eye.

"Be diligent to present yourself approved to God, a worker who does not need to be ashamed, rightly dividing the word of truth" (2 Tim. 1:15). This was Paul's advice to Timothy and to us. Timothy was a young preacher who Paul had taken under his wing to mentor and train. What really got my attention was the phrase, *rightly divide*.

There was an Old Covenant, the covenant of the law. And then there became a New Covenant, the covenant of grace. Exactly when did the change happen? And how do we distinguish or rightly divide passages of scripture, the *word of truth*, as to which covenant they apply? Jesus spoke of a dividing line between the old and the new. "Do you suppose that I came to give peace on earth? I tell you, not at all, but rather division. For from now on five in one house will be divided; three against two, and two against three. Father will be divided against son, mother against daughter, mother-in-law against her daughter-in-law, and daughter-in-law against her mother-in-law" (Luke 12:51–53).

Jesus was a Jew, and He came to preach to the Jewish people who were brought up in the traditions of the Old Covenant. The Law of Moses was where these people focused. This was a performance-based covenant. If a person did all the right things, God would bless him. If a person did something wrong, God would punish him. Of course, no one could satisfy all the requirements of the law. We all need a Savior—Jesus. "Do not think that I came to destroy the Law or the Prophets. I did not come to destroy but to fulfill" (Matt. 5:17). His life and then His death on the cross satisfied all the requirements of the law for all of us once and for all.

This New Covenant of grace was radically different. "Knowing that a man is not justified by the works of the law but by faith in Jesus Christ" (Gal. 2:16). It took the attention off of what a person did and put the attention on what a person believed and what Jesus did for us. "For by grace you have been saved through faith, and that not of yourselves; it is the gift of God" (Eph. 2:8). "For God so loved the world that He gave His only begotten Son, that whosoever believes in Him should not perish but have everlasting life" (John 3:16).

Where is the dividing line in scripture? There is a page in my Bible right after the last chapter in Malachi and right before the first chapter of Matthew. On this page it simply says, "New Testament." That is still not the dividing line between the Old and New Covenants. In a court proceeding, whatever the judge decrees take affect when he strikes the gavel. There should be a date on any contract—sometimes even a timestamp. After that moment in time, the contract takes effect. The New Covenant of grace was ratified by the blood of Jesus. "For if that first covenant had been faultless, then no place would have been sought for a second" (Heb. 8:7). "In that He says, 'A new covenant,' He has made the first obsolete. Now what is becoming obsolete and growing old is ready to vanish away" (Heb. 8:13).

In each of the Gospels, there is a verse describing the moment that Jesus died (Matt. 27:50, Mark 15:37, Luke 23:46, and John 19:30). Depending on the translation, these verses will say, "Jesus gave up the Ghost," or "Yielded up His Spirit," or "Breathed His last." He died. At that moment, the New Covenant took effect for all who believe in Jesus. This is the Gospel in a nutshell. Sin is the breaking of any of the laws or commandments listed in the Old Testament. There is a penalty for sin, and we were all guilty. Jesus took the rap for us. He sacrificed Himself to pay the full price for all mankind's sin. The Old Covenant required perfect adherence to over six hundred laws and regulations. The New Covenant requires us to believe in Jesus.

To this day this is a challenging concept even for people who were not raised Jewish. In the town where I live, the Ten Commandments are posted in front of our old courthouse. This is great, and an awesome reminder of God's holy character and the standards we should all live by. But now our eternal life is not subject to the Old Covenant of the law. It is good to obey God's laws. He has laid out many principles and standards that, if followed, will help us live a fruitful life. To not lie, cheat, steal, or kill other people is a good thing. This will help us avoid hurting ourselves and others and keep us from suffering civil prosecution. But our salvation with God comes through faith in what Jesus has done.

It is no longer a matter of what I have to do or not do. It's all about what Jesus has done. When a person hears the good news of the Gospel and receives Jesus as his Lord and Savior, he is saved. He is righteous in God's sight. His spirit has been reborn and perfect. His appearance does not change (except for the smile). His thoughts and emotions only begin to change at that moment. He is still subject to the urges and temptations of the flesh. But flesh is just what we live in temporarily. We are spirits that live forever.

In this new life, we might begin going to church and we might begin reading the Bible. This also is great. But this is where a lot of confusion can come about also. This is where rightly dividing the Word is so important. The principles expressed in the Old Testament are very good and useful, but that is the Old Covenant. We must be very careful about anything that says we have to do this or have to do that; or we can't do this or can't do that. This may be very good advice, but our salvation is not contingent upon our performance. Never forget that we are saved by grace through our faith in Jesus Christ. There is nothing that we can do to earn that grace, or to position ourselves to receive grace. It is not a reward; it is a gift. Our response should simply be extreme gratitude.

"And this is His commandment; that we should believe on the name of His Son Jesus Christ and love one another as He gave us commandment" (1 John 3:23). That is our commandment in the New Covenant—that we believe and love. If we love people, we will not lie to them, steal from them, or try to hurt them in any way. If we love God, we will want to honor Him and live a life that might please Him. But salvation and all the blessings of God are ours simply by believing in Jesus. "With the heart one believes unto righteousness" (Rom. 10:10). Our trust should be in what He has already done for us and not in what we might do.

The dividing line in our hearts should be centered on love. This is why we have been warned repeatedly not to judge other people. "Judge not, that you be not judged" (Matt. 7:1). "For whoever shall keep the whole law, and yet stumble in one point, he is guilty of all. For He who said, 'Do not commit adultery,' also said, 'Do not murder.' Now if you do not commit adultery, but you do murder, you have become a transgressor of the law. So speak and so do as those who will be judged by the law of liberty. For judgment is without mercy to the one who has shown no mercy. Mercy triumphs over judgment" (James 2:10–13). We have been shown mercy by God. We must show mercy to others. But our trust should be in what He has already done for us and not in what we might do.

A good understanding of the simplicity of the Gospel of grace helps when reading the Bible. "Now behold, one came and said to

Him, 'Good Teacher, what good shall I do that I may have eternal life?' So He said to him, 'Why do you call Me good? No one is good but One that is God. But if you want to enter into life, keep the commandments.' He said to Him, 'Which ones?' Jesus said, 'You shall not murder, you shall not commit adultery, you shall not steal, you shall not bear false witness, honor your father and your mother, and you shall love your neighbor as yourself.' The young man said to Him, 'All these things I have kept from my youth. What do I still lack?' Jesus said to him, 'If you want to be perfect, go sell what you have and give to the poor, and you will have treasure in heaven; and come follow Me'" (Matt. 19:16–21).

Many are confused by passages like this. The question was, "What must I *do*?" And then Jesus quoted the law. Many have taken this to mean that we all must *do* this. After all, it's what Jesus says. It's in the New Testament. But Jesus had not gone to the cross yet and all were still under the Old Covenant at that time. This particular scenario really points to Jesus as the only way to eternal life. Since no one has or can obey all the commandments like this person falsely claimed that he had.

Another source of confusion comes from the truth that God does not change. "Jesus Christ is the same yesterday, today and forever" (Heb. 13:8). God has not changed, but our relationship with Him has. All the statutes of the law illustrate His holy nature. It was never expected that anyone would actually live up to that standard, and to date, no one ever has except Jesus. It was God's purpose that the law would lead people to Jesus.

When rightly divided, the Bible becomes the most wonderful love story ever told. It is all about a loving God. "God is love" (1 John 4:8). It is a story about how He made a way for us to be part of His family. "Behold what manner of love the Father has bestowed on us, that we should be called the children of God" (1 John 3:1). It is a story about how wild and rebellious people can find redemption through simply believing in Jesus and what He has done for us.

The Word, when rightly divided, reassures us that God loves us and wants to bless us. And all these blessings are available through faith in Jesus. Whenever anyone preaches that we have to do this or can't do that, pointing to the law, they are not rightly dividing the Word. We must believe in Jesus and have faith in His Word. Everything flows from the knowledge of His love for us. When we realize how much He loves us and all people, we love all people. When we realize how much He has forgiven us, we forgive other people. Our performance is not the factor, God's love is.

"Stand fast therefore in the liberty by which Christ has made us free, and do not be entangled again with a yoke of bondage" (Gal. 5:1). The Old Covenant law brings entanglement and bondage. The New Covenant of grace brings liberty. We must rightly divide the Word and rightly divide our thoughts. Do they bring entanglement and condemnation, or do they bring us to the liberty of God's grace through Jesus? The Word, when rightly divided, may bring correction, but it will always bring hope, joy, and peace.

About the Author

Growing up in a middle-class suburban environment, John studied chemistry and engineering at a California university. John was not brought up with any religious training but was immersed in the culture and philosophies of the 1960s and 1970s. With a passion for understanding, he found these philosophies shallow and unsatisfying. Then he met Jesus.

Walking away from the party life of his youth, John found real truth in the Bible. For the last thirty years, he has led worship, written songs, and taught and ministered in churches, homeless shelters, and in prisons. He has no affiliation with any particular denominations or religious schools of thought—only that the Bible is the Word of God and the only source of real truth. His desire is to share this truth uncluttered with religious commentary.

Printed in the USA
CPSIA information can be obtained
at www.ICGtesting.com
CBHW021406050824
12617CB00065B/398